Problems in primary education

Problems in primary education

R. F. Dearden
Reader in the Philosophy of Education
University of London Institute of Education

Routledge & Kegan Paul
London, Henley and Boston

372.01

D34p

103528

2 an. 1978

First published in 1976
by Routledge & Kegan Paul Ltd
39 Store Street,
London WC1E 7DD
Broadway House,
Newtown Road,
Henley-on-Thames,
Oxon RG9 1EN and
9 Park Street,
Boston, Mass. 02108, USA
Set in IBM Press Roman by
Express Litho Service (Oxford)
and printed in Great Britain by
Redwood Burn Ltd
Trowbridge and Esher

ISBN 0 7100 8363 7 (c)
ISBN 0 7100 8364 5 (p)

The Students Library of Education has been designed to meet the needs of students of Education at Colleges of Education and at University Institutes and Departments. It will also be valuable for practising teachers and educationists. The series takes full account of the latest developments in teacher-training and of new methods and approaches in education. Separate volumes will provide authoritative and up-to-date accounts of the topics within the major fields of sociology, philosophy and history of education, educational psychology and method. Care has been taken that specialist topics are treated lucidly and usefully for the non-specialist reader. Altogether, the Students Library of Education will provide a comprehensive introduction and guide to anyone concerned with the study of education, and with educational theory and practice.

This collection of papers is a sequel to Dr Dearden's *The Philosophy of Primary Education* by which he established himself as one of the leading authorities in this field. It differs from his previous book in that it does not deal throughout with purely philosophical matters, but attempts, on occasions, to formulate lower-level principles for the guidance of practice in schools. He distinguishes between the level of principles to guide practice and the level of 'the commentaries available by way of explanation and evaluation of those guiding principles from the various disciplines which constitute the study of education'. His hope is that his return to practical principles, which were somewhat neglected during the process of differentiating the educational disciplines in the 1960s, does not lose sight of these 'foundation' disciplines which raise the discussion of practical principles 'above the level of subjective opinion-swapping and the comparison of personal impressions'.

This book is unlike most collections in that the majority of the papers have not appeared in print before. They are revisions of lectures and talks that Dr Dearden has given at various centres round the country during the past few years. Only the last four papers are reprints of papers previously published. The topics range from the very abstract — e.g. the papers on 'Aims and principles' and 'The concept of teaching', to the very concrete — e.g. 'What is the integrated day?', 'Competition in education' and 'Reading and research'.

This book, therefore, should be of interest not just to those interested in the philosophy of education but to anyone interested in the practical problems of primary education. Dr Dearden's previous experience as a teacher in a junior school, together with his philosophical training and experience as a teacher of philosophy of education, make him pre-eminently fitted to write such a book.

R.S.P.

Contents

Contents

Preface

Three broad levels of thought can usefully be distinguished in looking at schools: first, the concrete detail of moment to moment choice and decision, which inevitably dominates the mind of the inexperienced teacher; second, the general principles which are, or ought to be, guiding detailed practice; and third, the commentaries available by way of explanation and evaluation of those guiding principles from the various disciplines which constitute the study of education. So-called 'educational theory' may cover both the second and the third of these levels: both principles and their background in the disciplines. At one time, educational theory was almost wholly a discussion at the second level, without much differentiated attention being given to the disciplines of educational sociology and psychology, or the philosophy and the history of education. Then the emphasis shifted to a heavy concentration on the disciplines, with the discussion of practical principles being largely ignored. Very recently, this academically more respectable but pragmatically suspect emphasis has in turn met with much criticism.

Hopefully, this evolution will reveal itself in retrospect as having been a dialectical progression in which a return was made to the discussion of practical principles, but without forgetting or losing sight of the 'foundation' disciplines which raise that discussion above the level of subjective opinion-swapping and the comparison of personal impressions. Anyway, the present book is offered in that hope. Its arguments move freely between levels two and three, without confinement by twinges of purist conscience. Not to attempt any discussion at level two is to leave an unfortunate void in educational discussion. It is also to head for a divorce in the shaky marriage between theory and practice. If, however, we still wish to be purist, then let us first be sure that we are not merely being timid, and playing safe by living wholly inside our subject identities.

Though I have chosen as a title 'problems in *primary* education', really much of the discussion would be equally relevant to secondary interests. But sometimes one has to be specific about the age of the children or the particular practice or institution that one has in mind, and then it is to the primary school that I have turned. In selecting the 'problems' that I have selected, I have tried to avoid merely repeating what I have already said elsewhere. Principally, this has meant avoiding overlap with my own previous book *The Philosophy of Primary Education,* which is also published in this Students Library series. I have also refrained from reprinting articles of mine already available in *Education and the Development of Reason,* which I edited together with P. H. Hirst and R. S. Peters, and which is now available subdivided into three smaller volumes. The four chapters included here which are reprints of previously published articles have been lightly edited to fit them better into the present book, and also to remove any dated references. But the first five chapters are new. They are the constantly modified outcome of lectures which I have regularly given at various teachers' centres, colleges of education and universities. I am grateful for the stimulation which these occasions have afforded, and for the comments and inquiries to which they have led.

R.F.D.

Acknowledgments

The first five chapters of this book have not appeared before. The latter part of chapter 6, on learning by discovery, is reprinted from the recently founded journal *Education 3–13*, vol. 1, no. 1, April 1973, with the permission of Collins Educational of Glasgow. Chapter 7, on the integrated day, is reprinted from *The Integrated Day in Theory and Practice*, edited by Jack Walton and published in 1971 as the outcome of a conference at Exeter University. Acknowledgment is due to Ward Lock Educational Ltd., of London. Chapter 8 originally bore the unchosen and somewhat cumbrous title 'Curricular Implications of Developments in the Teaching of Reading'. It was subsequently published in 1967 by Cassell, of London, in a book called *The Second International Reading Symposium*, edited by J. Downing and Amy L. Brown. The final chapter, on competition, is reprinted from the *Proceedings of the Philosophy of Education Society of Great Britain*, vol. 6, no. 1, January 1972, by permission of Blackwell and Mott, of Oxford.

Part one

Aims and principles

Chapter one

Who should determine aims?

Schools are rather special places with special purposes. They are places which have been specially arranged and intended so that people may learn things, and may do so under the directive guidance of teachers. Schools do other things as well, of course, some of which are also done by other institutions. But the essential point and purpose of a school, the feature which distinguishes it from a recreation ground, factory, restaurant or whatever, is that it is specially arranged and intended for learning to take place under the directive guidance of teachers. This is no less true of our primary schools, or of our first and middle schools, than it is of schools of any other kind.

This is not to deny, of course, that schools do have, in varying degree, wider human and welfare functions. They may be convenient points at which to make available certain medical services, for example. But if teachers lose sight of their primary purpose, then very likely their energies will be dissipated in roles which are too diffuse for effectiveness and for which they are in any case untrained. The principle should not be that a teacher must be equally concerned with his pupils in every aspect of their existence, but that he should be primarily concerned with such aspects as bear upon (sometimes indeed even make impossible) his role as a teacher. Rather than attempting to be a doctor, social worker, magistrate, psychiatrist and so on, a more modest and realistic claim would be to be able to recognize when someone else's expertise is needed. The point here is to distinguish between recognizing that effective teaching requires an awareness of much more than goes on in one's classroom, and losing sight of relevance to teaching in that widening awareness.

Logically, then, the first question to ask about a school would be what the people going there, the pupils or students, should be learning. If nothing much is learned, or if what is learned is of little value, then the place may possibly be doing the job of some other institution rather well, but the distinctive purpose in having a school will have been lost, or defeated. The quality and extent of what is learned there form the heart of a good school. This is not to imply, however, that what is learned should be confined to facts and skills, very important though these are. Interests, attitudes, habits, virtues and relationships may be just as important, perhaps even more important, items of learning which the teachers properly set themselves as aims.

What, then, should the pupils in our primary schools be learning? What, in general terms, should we be aiming at? What is success and what is failure in the way of learning in a primary school? As soon as such logically first questions are asked, and squarely faced, the difficulty of answering them becomes apparent. For it seems unlikely that anyone could himself be sufficiently widely educated, sufficiently aware of the natures and differences of primary school children, and sufficiently versed in the practical possibilities of a school's situation to be able to form an adequate and comprehensive judgment. So difficult is this question, in fact, that it has been customary to let tradition settle it. Attention can then be given to the much easier and more businesslike questions of method and of organization.

But schools are unlike business enterprises in many ways. Those who operate businesses may set before themselves as their primary goal the maximizing of profits. This is a goal that seems unambiguous and which naturally and immediately shifts attention to the practicalities of how the thing is to be done. But with schools, concerned as they should be to give an education, there is nothing corresponding which is so clear and unambiguous as maximizing profits. It is irrational, therefore, to be fully preoccupied with questions of means when the ends are genuinely so open to debate. And indeed various circumstances have, over the course of the last decade or so, put strong pressure on those who work in schools to reflect upon their aims. There has been such a spate of innovation, whether originated, pressed, canvassed, carried out or only heard of, that the need for some broad and overall perspective has been felt as perhaps never before. And indeed, to return to the business analogy for a moment, even the apparently clear-cut aim of profitable production in business has become less clear-cut as job-satisfaction for employees and wider social responsibilities affecting the public interest are brought into the reckoning.

The Plowden Report on aims

Since a logical priority over other questions attaches to the question of aims, and since the innovations of the last decade have given a special urgency to that question, it was surprising that the Plowden Report was so unsatisfactory on this point. The relevant brief chapter[1] gives a strong impression that it was touch-and-go whether to regard the question as worth raising at all. There were, in fact, three reasons for hesitation which deserve attention, and which do have some force.

The first reason was that general statements of aim are often rather loosely connected with the actual practice of teachers. This is quite true. Grand-sounding phrases such as 'our cultural heritage', or 'the full development of each child's potential', may have their place on speech day platforms, in prospectuses, or in students' essays, but when it comes to the crunch at nine-fifteen on Monday morning, such notions are apt to flee to the remotest corners of consciousness, or beyond. Then again, and it is not an unconnected second point, general statements of aim are apt to be rather platitudinous. Everyone is apt to agree with them, which is a sure sign that they are nerveless, or empty of content. As soon as you approach something with more bite in it, such as someone's assertion that the use of competition is a good educational principle, consensus vanishes. Agreement and platitude do tend to go together where aims are concerned.

Each of these objections — that general statements of aim are loosely connected with practice and that they are apt to be platitudinous — is well made, but such objections are relative to those sorts of general statements. Aims do not have to have this unsatisfactory character. If they often do have, then that is surely a reason for doing better, not for abandoning the whole enterprise in a blind concentration on more limited and logically subordinate questions of method and organization.

But the Plowden Report's third reason for hesitation was more interesting. It was that successful teachers and headteachers are often unable to state their aims. The implication is the obvious one that if their degree of success is achievable without stating or formulating aims, then what is the practical value of that difficult enterprise, especially for people who are already hard-pressed with claims on their time and energy? Yet surely it is not being claimed that these very successful practitioners are literally aimless in what they do? Surely they do more than radiate sunny personalities and spread cheer around? Surely they *achieve* something worthwhile in the way of learning, and not just by accident? Without aims, what are the criteria of success and failure by which to judge one's efforts? If we have aims, our energies are released and purposefully directed, and we are more likely to hit the mark. What we do is more likely to be consistent, and gaps and omissions in what we do are more easily recognized. We can take our bearings rather more clearly when confronted by choices of priority and by suggested innovations.

In reply to this, it might be said that the achievement of aims is quite possible without teachers having to think about them, provided that what they do is tightly controlled by some source of authoritative direction. Many educational systems are indeed organized on that pattern, and those who wish teachers' initial training to be confined to supplying immediate classroom survival equipment are cast in the same mould. Nevertheless, this kind of external authoritative direction was very far from what the Plowden Committee had in mind, or would have been sympathetic towards.

A way forward here is to distinguish between *having* aims, and being able to *state* them, with its associated intellectual operations of formulation and justification. Plowden's 'successful practitioners' doubtless had aims, but they did not have the ability to communicate them very satisfactorily. In much the same way, we all of us use words with confidence and accuracy which we would nevertheless be hard-pressed to define. Again, a newspaper editor may run a highly successful newspaper, yet be unable to articulate just what are his criteria of 'news', or exactly what effect he wants to produce. To use a phrase of Polanyi's, there is 'tacit knowledge' as well as knowledge which is available in a clearly articulated verbal form.

But there are some respects in which Plowden's successes would have been less successful, just because they could not state, and consequently could not justify, their aims. They would have been unsuccessful, not as teachers of children, but as teachers of teachers. They would also have had problems in explaining to parents, or to school visitors of whatever kind, just what it was that they were trying to achieve. The latter inadequacy may be frustrating or embarrassing, but the former is worse in making others dependent on one's authority. It was in fact headteachers who were principally the subject of discussion. If a headteacher cannot communicate his aims and principles, his 'philosophy' if you like, then his staff will be made very dependent on his judgment. The least that one might claim here is that the teaching of teachers would at least be expedited if the point behind it could be formulated and stated, justified or discussed. But so long as 'successful practitioners' have aims without being able to formulate them, they will be apt to remain either the sole beneficiaries of this knowledge, or else be forced into giving detailed direction to others in a way which is at best very slow to create independence.

The school's autonomy in determining aims

An assumption made so far has been that it should be the teachers, led by the headteacher, who should determine the aims of a school. Yet the slightest acquaintance with the educational systems of other countries, or indeed with the earlier history of our own system, is sufficient to put that assumption in question. Is it justifiable that the schools should have such a degree of autonomy? On the face of it, there are several other groups who might have as good a claim, or even a better one, for example the parents, an appointed panel of 'experts', or even the pupils themselves. The staffs of schools may disagree amongst themselves over the degree to which headteachers should make unilateral decisions on policy, but should the question of aims properly be settled in the school at all?

Whatever discretion in this aspect may in practice be allowed to the schools, as a matter of law it would seem that the education authorities have the right to determine aims. They are charged with providing an education which is desirable in view of pupils' 'different ages, abilities and aptitude'. Within living memory it was not unknown for authorities

7

to require the submission for approval of detailed minute-by-minute timetables. The greater discretion of recent years, extending as it has to the allocation of finance, may prove to have been a phase only. Certainly authorities have issued to schools directives on the teaching of French as well as the eating of sandwiches, on sex education as well as on heating, and on corporal punishment as well as on staff quotas. Some energetic and even visionary chief education officers and advisors have put their stamp on whole counties, while others speak of the urgent need for methods of evaluating performance. Fully to comprehend the untidiness and uncertainty of this situation, one has to try describing it to a foreigner, preferably one from a very neat and tidy system.

There are, I think, three main reasons why this recent tradition of school autonomy might be questioned. The first of these reasons arises from the mobility of the adult population, coupled with the diversity of practices in schools. The consequence of this is that children of mobile parents may suffer and become confused through the diversity of practices and expectations which they meet. They begin reading with traditional orthography, only to move school to one where the initial teaching alphabet is used. Similar experiences occur in relation to the learning of a foreign language (which may be productive of problems for the secondary school) and also in relation to the content and methods of mathematics teaching. These problems may to a lesser degree occur within schools as well as between schools, if teachers do not or are not required to co-operate closely. Something can be, and to a varying extent is, done to alleviate these consequences by local consultation and agreement between headteachers, or an acceptable ruling can be given by the local education authority. But a degree of unwanted and unintended consequence remains, so that the case for school autonomy has to show that it can outweigh, even if it cannot wholly remove, these disadvantages.

The second attack would be on the teachers' competence. I do not have in mind the teacher near retirement who will not inconvenience himself by troublesome changes, or the school which is quite unresponsive to legitimate parental complaint. We are concerned here with the general case. Every system produces schools of varying quality as judged by the system's own criteria. The present attack would be directed at the limited knowledge and limited abilities of teachers in relation to the massive literature of research and expert discussion which now exists internationally on schooling and education. How can an individual teacher in a classroom embrace all of this in the scope of his judgment? Even the headteacher, hopefully with more time to stand back, reflect and compare, cannot keep abreast of every relevant piece of curriculum development, every new publication and project, or the findings of experts who have the time and resources to draw widely and think deeply. The quasi-Platonic solution, widely adopted elsewhere, is therefore to settle questions of aim and principle, even of detailed curriculum organization and teaching method, by groups of relevant experts. We shall return to this, the most substantial attack on school autonomy later.

Yet a third attack might be from the direction of the parents. They might question the teachers' *right* to be the architects of their children's education. Is it not sufficient invasion of parental rights that children should, in effect, be compelled to attend school, without any further exclusion from a say in what the children should be taught? There are certainly many ways in which parents can be encouraged to take a greater interest in their children's education, and to take a more active part in helping and supporting the schools, but should they not determine the aims and policy? Let us consider first this parental claim.

If right is grounded in competence, then where school learning is concerned parents have a weaker case than the teachers. If they did not, there would be something sadly wrong with the teachers and indirectly with their training. The answer then would be to institute reforms designed to make teachers more competent, rather than to hand over to the parents. As things are, teachers have been through a selection process and have been trained. To this training they add experience and further in-service work. They are also in a better position than are parents to assess institutional possibilities and practicalities. And they work, not in a vacuum, but properly subject to very many pressures, such as the scrutiny of their professional colleagues, the limits of children's co-operation, the promotional policies current in the district, and the comments of visiting inspectors and advisers. Most parents, by contrast, have only their own dimly recollected and possibly idealized schooldays as a basis on which to judge. To this argument based on greater competence can be added the longer-term interest of teachers in the success of their school, whereas parental interest is typically and very naturally more transient and particular.

Assuming that parental control would be in the hands of elected representatives, rather than in the hands of the parent body as a whole, then there are well-known dangers over securing a true representation of parental opinion. Less commonly noticed is the point that it is not only the parents who have an interest in the schools, but the whole community. This interest derives both from the fact that the education service is the largest single consumer of local government finance, collected from parents and non-parents alike, and also from the fact that the pupils are participant members of a wider community which has to live with them, and in the productive work of which they will ultimately have to share. If a democratic argument demanding accountability is pressed in support of a parental right to control the school, then that argument must allow for accountability much more widely than simply to the parents. As things are, such accountability is formally provided through the managers, the local education authority and the local and national electoral systems. Wide accountability is thus already present, even if insufficiently strongly so in some people's view.

On the question of parental control, the Plowden Report would seem nearly to have got it right. That report advocated much more interaction between teachers and parents, both in help and support for the school from parents, and in greater openness of the school to parental inquiry, curiosity and sometimes complaint. Behind all of this lay the perception that children's attitudes to learning are crucial to the success of the school, and that parental interest or the lack of it importantly determines those attitudes. But on the question of aims and policy, both for conduct and for curriculum, Plowden was clear that the school should be self-determining. That is not to say that parents should never, no matter how extraordinary the circumstances, put pressure on a school to change or else justify itself. But between that pressure and actual policy should come the school's own professional, and one hopes principled, judgment, based on competence. And if disagreement is too deep for that to be an arrangement satisfactory to a parent, then there should be a parental right to change to another school.[2]

The determination of aims by experts[3]

The question we are considering is whether primary schools should continue to enjoy the degree of autonomy that they now have in determining their aims and general policy. A second possible claimant to that right can easily be imagined, since in most countries in the world such an alternative already exists. This alternative would be for panels of 'experts' to be appointed who would draw up curricular principles and guidelines, perhaps embodying a considerable degree of detail as to what should be done and when. Basically the argument would be the Platonic one that the wisest should rule. And since so much of the case for the schools as against the parents as the agency to determine aims has depended on an appeal to superior competence, it surely only requires an agency which is in turn superior in competence to the teachers for the determination of aims to move out of the schools and upward to that agency. Such an agency (a panel or committee of experts) could be drawn from the most experienced teachers as well as from other groups, but for most teachers it would be their source of pedagogic direction. And not only would it claim greater competence, but it would also introduce that uniformity of practice which the geographical mobility of parents makes so desirable.

It would be no objection to such centralized direction to say that there could not be any such competent body, since education rests on value-judgments and value-judgments are all subjective anyway (i.e. a matter of personal preference). If that were true, it would not help the schools, since their preferences could then in turn claim no superiority over the supposed 'experts', or over the parents, or indeed over the preferences of the children themselves. Schools would be reduced to expressing what was simply a rival subjectivity. On the other hand, if value-judgments are not just personal preferences, backed only by more or less power, then some people will certainly be better judges than others. An attempt then to select the best judges to determine aims would seem a highly justifiable procedure to adopt. The experts need not be Platonic philosopher-kings in touch with the absolute and final truth; they need only be the best judges that can be found.

There is thus a strong case for centralized control, at least when an educational system is abstractly considered. In the present concrete historical context, however, there may be more to be said for the actual

11

system that we have: a degree of autonomy surrounded and limited by formal authority, pressure and persuasion. But to make a case for the actual would not be to defend it unconditionally, or to defend it against all future eventualities. It would have to be a case made conditional on several important contingencies.

Can a case be made, then, for a high degree of school autonomy as regards aims and policy? One consideration of some importance would be that the staff on the spot are in the best position to devise a programme for the children in a particular school and in a particular area. Only they have the detailed knowledge to adapt and innovate in accordance with individual and local variations in circumstance. As Sir Karl Popper has pointed out, you can always centralize power but you cannot always centralize the knowledge which would be relevant to its exercise. Devolution is therefore more than a charming idea: it has a rational basis in certain limits on the distribution of knowledge. Any educational system, even the most centrally directive, must recognize this at some point. As so often, the question will be one of degree. But this first consideration can be reinforced by reference to the complexity of judgments about aims. Such judgments logically rest on psychological and sociological considerations, administrative feasibilities and resources, value-judgments about learning as well as working relationships and institutional practicalities. 'Experts' normally become experts by taking a specialized interest in one part of one such area, which does not necessarily fit them, and may even unfit them, for the more holistic judgment which a decision of practical policy requires. But it is the teacher who in the end has unavoidably to attempt such an holistic judgment however inadequately it may be as judged by an ideal composite standard.

A second consideration relevant to the case is that devolution is more than a charming idea in another way. Through giving the freedom, responsibility and trust necessary for the exercise of autonomy, important and valuable motivations are frequently engendered. People feel more committed to and involved in something which they have had a hand in designing or deciding. They will give more of themselves and of their time and effort, with correspondingly greater satisfaction and fulfilment, and we may suppose that a better quality of recruit will be attracted by such an opportunity. On the other hand, a system which mistrusts people, which closely prescribes what they will do and which regularly inspects them to see that they are doing it, will certainly succeed in diverting much energy into defeating that system.

Yet a third consideration is that school autonomy makes possible valuable innovations though admittedly it also makes possible some fashion-following and gimmickry. Not only does it provide schools with the opportunity to originate new practices, but it also makes the further dissemination of new practices something freely adopted and therefore more committed. Devising beneficial innovations quite outside the schools, which latter are then lined up as recipient targets for these benefits, has a history of resistance and half-hearted acquiescence to count against it. And if the reluctance of some schools to use their autonomy to much evident advantage is a count in favour of centralized direction, a danger in such centralization may be recognized in its making educational policy an instrument of political party policy. It is impossible to 'keep education out of politics', but the *political* decision, made in a liberal tradition, to decentralize control even down to school level has much to commend it.

The criterion by which this question is to be decided, I suggest, is a threefold one: Are the children's educational interests best served by the proposed system? Does it represent good value to the community in return for the community's investment of resources? Does it best provide for the professional job-satisfaction of those who are to staff it? Of course, there is no guarantee of perfect compatibility between these three requirements, but it is a defensible judgment, in the present concrete historical context, that a system which gives a large degree of autonomy to the school in determining its aims and policy is to be preferred.

Why add the historical qualification? It is included for several reasons. Clearly the system envisaged would not be justifiable if teachers were themselves too uneducated or too unwilling to turn to advantage the trust placed in them. A good level of education is therefore presupposed, as also is a willingness to profit from experience and from further in-service training. A further desirability is that there should be local co-operation between schools to minimize any confusion caused by a mobile child population and by failing to complement the purposes of the secondary schools. Third, it has to be recognized that basing a right on competence implies different degrees of competence in different teachers, deriving from differences in

13

experience and the capacity to profit from it. This in turn implies the possibility of a justifiable authority structure in schools and its acceptance as such.

De-schooling and learner autonomy

Whereas until recently almost no-one would have suggested that the control over their learning should rest with children themselves, nowadays this suggestion is very far from outlandish. A. S. Neill for a long time urged something like this, but at least his pupils were in attendance. Now, under the attacks of Ivan Illich and others,[4] compulsory attendance has itself been radically questioned, and indeed strongly opposed. Society should apparently be 'de-schooled'. The school-churches of that modern secular religion, education, should be disestablished and their hateful teacher-priests presumably should all be defrocked. Instead, there should be a rather vaguely outlined system of 'learning webs' to which children go (or do not go) as they wish, according to their felt needs. In practice, of course, compulsory schooling has now celebrated its centenary, during which time the school leaving age has been progressively raised to twelve, fourteen, fifteen, and now sixteen, with the prospect in some minds at least of a further raising to seventeen and even eighteen. General principles, however, cannot reach to such particular decisions as exact ages. But why is Illich so radically opposed to the general principle of compulsory schooling? And has his argument any validity?

Basic to Illich's case is his distinction between convivial and manipulative institutions. 'Convivial' institutions, such as the postal system, telephones, markets, parks and pathways, are at the service of the user of them. They wait to be used and are, as it were, content not to be used. They are tools firmly subordinated to our self-determined purposes. 'Manipulative' institutions, by contrast, such as motor manufacturers, organized medicine and organized religion, seek positively to manipulate our desires and self-concepts in such a way that we serve the purposes of the institution. It defines our needs in relation to its product, or 'service'. Whereas a market stallholder may press his tomatoes on me as I pass, but otherwise leaves me alone, a motor manufacturer will subtly play on my imagination so that my hopes and fears, my judgments of personal success and failure, even my sexuality, are bound up with, defined and evaluated in terms of his product and its possession by me.

The application of this distinction to education is that schools are said to be manipulative institutions. And they are said to be so broadly in two main ways. First, schools are so closely interlocked with consumer-based industrial and commercial life that the requirements of that system distort the activities of the school in a way which is inimical to a concern for education. Schools function to select and grade for the job-roles which the society has created. They teach the kind of social control in large groups which industrial and commercial organizations require. They motivate pupils with such extrinsic incentives as grades and bits of paper, so preparing them for the extrinsic motivation of money which is necessary to keep society's roles functioning.

But, second, schools are said to be manipulative in subordinating education to the professional self-interest of teachers. Huge funds are being poured into schooling, with static or falling standards as the result, appallingly low cost-efficiency levels, and the only obvious beneficiaries being the teachers themselves and the school materials manufacturers. Schools are also said to teach that what they transmit is the only valuable learning, and that that learning indispensably requires teachers for it to be effective. Inequality of opportunity is rife in schools, since resources raised from the taxation of all sections of society are used in a way which gives most to the few ablest, whose schooling also lasts the longest. Furthermore, politicians use the schools to ease growing unemployment, through raising the school leaving age to keep more people off the labour market.

After recovering from this onslaught, what is to be made of it? Is this a travesty, a gross caricature, or just the simple truth about schools? Certainly there is much to distrust in Illich's argument. He grossly maligns the teaching profession by blurring the distinction between unintended consequences on the one hand, and deliberate manipulative intention on the other. He represents slight analogies as designed similarities. He chooses examples which are striking rather than representative, and which are often drawn heavily from the USA. He will say that schools perform their tasks with great economy when he wishes to reinforce an analogy with labour camps, but he will also say that they are most uneconomical if he is attacking their multiplicity of roles. In short, his criterion of relevance is that an analogy, statistic, instance or whatever will shock us into being appalled by schools and their activities. And, like all the best rhetoric, what he says contains enough truth to disturb.

But there are many points at which one can reasonably disagree with Illich. One can disagree that industry, commerce, medicine and education are so totally without benefit to the 'consumers' of their products, yet without asserting that any of these activities is an unmixed blessing. The assertion that schools are so tightly interlocked with the industrial-commercial system looks odd beside the opposite accusation that so much of schooling is 'irrelevant to life'. Again, to at least some degree, schools have shown themselves capable of reform and self-criticism which may put them out of step with powerful and organized social interests. Thus generalities can be met with generalities, and wholesale iconoclasm can be toned down to more limited complaint. There are, however, three considerations which need specially to be pressed in reply to Illich on education.

First of all, how serious is he in his respect for individual liberty? The convivial-manipulative distinction rests on a repugnance for the invasion of such liberty. Then suppose that most parents do not want to see society de-schooled, must not Illich de-family society as well? And in Illich's de-schooled society, are children's felt wants to be respected regardless of their educational consequences? In a de-schooled society it would only be a matter of *hope* that the 'learning web' was used as it was intended, or was used at all. Are adults to be free to set up webs of their own, untrained or not, and to ply for hire? Illich is too vague in his positive recommendations for the answers to these questions to .be clear, but one suspects that 'freedom' would be very much subject to Illich's idea of a 'good society'. If people do not want the Illich-approved forms of makeshift or low-technology transport, for example, then a demand for such is to be 'cultivated'. (But of course, that would not be 'manipulative', if it served his *good* ends!)

Second, a version of Illich's learners finding their way round a learning web already exists. We have it in the variety of resources available to an adult who wishes to take his education further, or to become proficient in some particular skill. For example, amongst such resources are certain television programmes, libraries, car-driving schools, extra-mural university classes, evening classes in photography, car maintenance and judo, horse-riding schools, foreign language schools, typing schools and the Open University. Adults may choose amongst these and other resources as they wish. But many adults choose to do little or nothing in these directions, and in some cases it is just as well because the 'resource' is concerned only to provide the least that it can for the highest possible price. Furthermore, adults who do choose amongst these resources do so as relatively educated adults, capable of understanding the nature and consequences of what they are doing and of exercising informed, autonomous choice. The central difficulty with this as a model for children's learning, however, is that children are not adults. So far are they from being like a wary adult choosing what to do with his spare time that, until they are taught to read, they would not even be able to read the literature advertising or informing them of the 'resources' and their whereabouts. In such a free situation, if the family is allowed by Illich to survive then we should see a new extreme of inequality of opportunity, for parents with the knowledge and sense of responsibility to see to it that their children were educated would indeed do that, whereas others would not. Differences between parents would magnify differences between their children.

The final consideration is that there may be something to be gained from a fresh look at the case for compulsory schooling, and thus for a curtailment of children's freedom to control their own learning. The starting point for such a review would be the unavoidable immaturity of children. Children have a personal identity which is continuous across the whole span of their lives. Thus they have interests which are not those of the present moment at all, but which derive from future stretches of their lives. But their present activities (and omissions) importantly affect, both advantageously and disadvantageously, those future interests. The younger that the children are, however, the less able are they either to appreciate or stably to act upon those future interests. If those interests are to be safeguarded, then someone who is more mature and stable must judge what those interests are and secure them on the child's behalf, though often indeed with his co-operation. The best people to do this will be people who can judge these interests, and who have a special knowledge of and concern for the child himself. And the best institutions we have so far devised to accomplish these objects are the family and the school, weight of responsibility shifting from the one to the other, and later gradually to the growing child himself of course.

The case for compulsory schooling, then, is first of all the frankly paternalistic one that what the school has to offer is too important for the child's future interests to be left entirely to his free choice whether he attends or not. Second, school is to secure some approximation to equality of opportunity in at least trying to make available to all children what otherwise would be available only to the children of wealthy and well-informed parents. Third, school is to protect children from forces which otherwise would be operative on them to their grave disadvantage, such as being sent out by their parents to work in ways which have as their only merit some small addition to the family income. Fourth, and this is counter to our liberal individualist tradition to some extent, the wider society has a legitimate interest in how children are taught and brought up, since they are members of that wider society. At the very least, this interest legitimately extends to a basic moral education and to the acquisition of such competences as will not make the adult that the child will become needlessly economically dependent on the rest of that society. The fact that we have to live together and work together has some legitimate bearing on children's activities.

Of course, even if such a case for compulsory schooling were valid, it would be valid only where schooling realities corresponded to that case. Actual schools are not all equally able to claim that they protect and further children's interests, or that they equalize certain opportunities, or that society's trust in them is well placed. There are schools which would be better closed, and indeed there are schools which are closed. But again, general principles cannot reach to every particularity. If the argument given above is valid, then it indicates some of the principles by which individual schools might be judged, and the directions in which some schools would need to reform.

Chapter two

Aims and objectives

An increasingly popular response to the problem of aims is to dismiss, as wrong-headed, thinking in such terms at all. It is not aims that we should be seeking to determine, so the argument will go, but objectives. Grandiose talk in terms of self-realization, happiness, developing potentials and the like should be abandoned. Even apparently more determinate aims, such as developing mathematical understanding, an appreciation of music, or problem-solving skills, are very little better. Instead of all such vague and general talk, we should instead be seeking to determine highly specific learning objectives, clearly stated in terms of the behavioural performances of which the pupil will be capable if we succeed in teaching him. We should 'operationalize' our objectives by stating the specific observable behaviours which will verify or falsify any claim to have taught successfully.

A powerful pressure in the direction of thinking in this new way comes from politicians and administrators who wish to apply to schooling ideas of productivity and cost-effectiveness. Is the paying community getting value for money from its schools and from its teachers? Why should teachers not be accountable to the community for their level of productivity in terms of learning brought about? And the pressure behind this line of thinking becomes all the more insistent when educational costs escalate, while educational standards apparently remain static, or are even thought to be falling. But if these insistent questions are to be answered, then visible and if possible measurable results in terms of learning will have to be evidenced. The proof of cost-efficiency will have to be publicly observable behavioural performances.

The thought-forms in terms of which these cost-efficiency questions are asked and answered are already available in the worlds of military training and commercial activity. It would be no use for the army simply to set itself to produce good soldiers, for what constitutes a 'good soldier'? One such constituent would be the ability to fire a rifle. But even that is far from specific enough for an efficient training programme to be mounted. More detailed behavioural objectives must first be pre-specified, such as the abilities to load, aim and fire a rifle, to handle it safely and, if the army is still what it was, no doubt to keep the rifle spotlessly clean. Similarly, if a commercial transport enterprise is set the objective of making a profit, that is still too vague. Something more specific, such as filling more unused off-peak capacity, must be set as the objective. This greater specificity of objective permits the clear formulation of well-chosen means, and lends itself to a clear statement of the criteria by which success is to be judged. Are more off-peak seats occupied as a result of the means taken to reach the objective? Are more bullseyes safely and speedily scored as a result of the military training programme? All that is needed is to apply the same general approach to education: specify your objectives as terminal behaviour, select your means (content, method and organization) accordingly, then test to evaluate your success. And the psychological testing and educational technology people represent an obvious interest-group who will be only too ready to give loud support and a vigorous thrust to this new policy.

This new look at the problem of aims is not just a return to the traditional injunction to 'state the aim of your lesson'. It cannot reasonably be doubted that teaching will benefit from the teacher's thinking about what he is doing and where he is going, and from his checking up on whether he is getting there. Teaching is a purposeful activity, and it will be the more effective the clearer the purpose. But what is new is that it is not teacher-intentions or teacher-purposes which are to be clarified, but learner-behaviour. It is not just that teachers should do some course planning, or careful forecasting, but that they should write down in detail the *pre-specified behaviours* which their pupils will evidence as a result of teaching. Pupil performance per pound spent is the new message.

The implementation of this approach is at present more evident in the USA than in Great Britain, and no doubt there are interesting reasons why that should be so. Perhaps the extreme so far reached down this road is 'performance contracting', in which children's learning is, as it were, put out to tender, and teacher-payment is made conditional on delivering the goods in the right quantity and at the right time. But already in Great Britain standard textbooks in the genre, such as Bloom's early *Taxonomy of Educational Objectives*[1] and the more recent variants on 'how to develop the curriculum', are gaining attention. So far as primary education is concerned, the effects are as yet slight, but the Science 5/13 teacher's book *With Objectives in Mind*[2] is perhaps an indication of what is to come, as are the statements of objectives in some recent mathematics textbooks. Are these the forerunners of an updated version of Robert Lowe's 'payment by results'? Perhaps they are. Perhaps they should be. But rather than speculate about the future, let us consider the validity of the objectives approach. How compelling is the case for this new response to the problem of aims?

Our knowledge of others' behaviour

An initial difficulty which is likely to be felt by anyone acquainted with recent work in philosophy concerns the idea of verifying educational success by reference to 'terminal behaviours', or 'behavioural performances'. The problem is not with the claim that we know about others' minds only through what might broadly be called their 'behaviour'. Indeed, that claim is probably correct. How else am I to know what you believe, feel, want, intend, or can do, if not through what I can observe of your behaviour? Admittedly, a knowledge of your past history and of the present situation as it affects you may be equally important clues to your mind, but behaviour has an indispensable place. Such dubious alternatives as telepathy and clairvoyance certainly would not serve the day-to-day needs of the teacher. But behavioural evidence is evidence for something distinguishable from that behaviour, and the relation between the evidence and that for which it may be the evidence is a source of difficulty for the objectives approach.

An extreme case is dreaming. Our behavioural evidence for attributing a particular dream to someone, even our evidence for attributing the process of dreaming at all, rests on the person's reports or confirmations when he wakes up. But what he then says is not the dream itself. It is the report of a recollected dream which occurred perhaps hours, days, or even years before. Here, the gap between mental process and behavioural evidence is clear enough. Now consider a smile. What sort of a smile is it? Is it the smile of genuine pleasure at seeing me in particular, or the crafty dissembling smile of the manipulator trying to put me off my guard, or the automatic smile of one who feels that his religion requires that everyone he meets should be smiled at, or is it no smile at all but merely a smile-like grimace at some accompanying pain or effort? Thus behavioural evidence can be very ambiguous. Where the behavioural evidence is strongest, if not conclusive, is with practical capacities. If I see someone swim the length of the baths, then unquestionably he can swim. If I watch someone jump ten feet, lift a hundredweight or repeatedly flip a pancake, then undoubtedly he can do these things. In cases such as these, there is no reasonable room for doubt once we are able to witness the behaviour. But in general, a distinction has to be drawn between *what it means* to refer a mental concept to a person, and *how we know,* on a given occasion, that the concept is applicable.

Because of this distinction between meaning and evidence, behaviour is in general ambiguously related to mind. A particular belief, or attitude, or desire of mine may be evidenced in enormously varied ways, some of them quite unpredictable and therefore not pre-specifiable, or it may be evidenced in no way at all. Diplomacy would not be such a guessing game if the other side's intentions, purposes, beliefs and desires were immediately transparent once we were able to gaze upon their behaviour. Behaviouristic attempts to spell out what it is to believe something, for example, have notoriously failed at that point where the relevant class of equivalent behaviours tails off with a vague 'and so on', or 'and that sort of thing'. In general mental states and activities are expressed in classes of behaviour which it is impossible completely to specify.

Just as something mental can be evidenced in a great variety of behaviours, so in reverse can a given piece of behaviour be evidence for a diversity of mental correlates. Consider a man running along the street. We see the running clearly enough. But is he trying to catch a train, hastening to make a purchase before the shops shut, trying to avoid the impending storm, escaping from a crime, engaging in vigorous exercise for his health's sake, warming himself on this cold morning, testing the robustness of his new shoes, practising for the weekend's athletics trials, or ...? This great variety of mentalistic descriptions, and more, may all be compatible with the running behaviour which we see. Behavioural evidence is ambiguous, though a knowledge of a person's past history and of the situational possibilities might rapidly narrow the range.

One reason for this ambiguity in behavioural evidence is that what people think, feel and do is not an isolated event but has its existence in relation to many other thoughts, feelings and actions. My belief that to-day is Tuesday is related to a whole system of beliefs about the sequence of days and their different patterns of activity. My feeling of anger is related to beliefs about others, their obstructiveness and the implications of all this for my wider purposes. My actions, too, typically have their place in a wider system of action and belief in which projects are progressively realized in constantly changing circumstances. Take a child who writes down an answer to a question calling for the perimeter of a given rectangle. That he has written something down is evident enough. But what else is? Did he guess or copy the answer? Did he solve the problem mechanically, according to a rule he has been taught, or did he solve it intelligently, by sorting out essentials and finding a way for the first time? Did he do it casually, or was he trying to do his best? Did he see it as a challenge or a bore? Answers to all of these questions are relevant if we are correctly to interpret the behavioural evidence.

The broad upshot of these points about behaviour is this. Human beings have a varied mental life of which their outward behaviour gives some evidence to others, thus enabling others to know what they are thinking, feeling or doing. But the relation between the two is rarely so simple as the relation between someone's having the capacity to swim and my knowing this from watching him do it. No behavioural evidence at all may be on offer. Deception is possible. The ways in which mentality may be behaviourally evidenced are impossible completely to specify, and conversely, even a specified piece of behaviour may be evidence of a great variety of mentalistic correlates involving reference to an elaborately interconnected system of beliefs, feelings and actions. Educationally, this means that pre-specifying detailed behavioural objections may be feasible enough for isolated physical or practical skills, such as doing a handstand or planing some wood. It will still have some feasibility if what we want is simply verbal responses to questions that we put. But the further we move from such relatively unambiguous bits of behaviour, the more impractical and unreliable this hard-headed search for certainty will become.

It is seen at its most absurd, perhaps, in connection with aesthetic education. For here, so much depends on images, associations, echoes, resonances, feelings and a mental hinterland of penumbral meaning that a 'behavioural objective' (perhaps: 'asks to hear the poem again') is as close to the educational heart of the matter as are shutting your eyes and putting your hands together to a deeply-felt belief in God. A crucial danger here is that the very heart of the matter may be debunked, or lost sight of, or even dismissed as 'not real', just because it is not overtly and unambiguously visible in behaviour. Thus if teachers are pressured to specify their behavioural objectives, either they will have to waste much time in deceitfully pretending to follow a fashion which they know to be anti-educational, or else they will actually yield to that pressure by narrowing their educational aims just to the bits of behaviour which will in fact fit in with the preconceptions of this approach. They will teach narrowly for the test, rather than broadly educate.

These difficulties over the concept of behaviour are not all. How, we may ask, are these objectives to be selected in the first place? We have only been told the form which they must take, but what of their content? What is to make an objective educationally worthwhile? Surely to answer these questions, appeal will have to be made once again to something like the despised and woolly aims in terms of which the enterprise of educating has traditionally been conceived. For education involves the endowment of a growing mind with an understanding and appreciation of a complex culture. It is not just the building up of a behavioural repertoire. Not only will such deplorably vague aims have to be reinstated, but their reinstatement will lead us constantly to recognize the inadequacy of pre-specified behavioural outcomes as an appropriate means of teaching for their achievement. Worse still, no school test of any sort could check on teaching which looks beyond the end of schooling for its ultimate success. On some matters, teachers have to be content with an unpredictable variety of chance clues and suggestive uncontrolled observations, or even with just a reasonable hope based on having done one's best by way of teaching. Too insistent a demand for hard, pre-specified, behavioural evidence would be destructively narrowing of any liberally conceived notion of education.

Again, we may well ask for evidence of the cost-efficiency of the cost-efficiency approach itself. Writing detailed lists of pre-specified behavioural objectives, and setting up tests for the attainment of each of them, would be incredibly time-consuming. Is it supposed to be perfectly obvious that this time is better spent than it would be in resting content with something less precise and then moving on to fresh learning? Of course, there would not be wanting those eager to 'help' the teacher here by devising schedules of objectives and by constructing suitable tests for them. This could become a growth industry overnight, once again without anyone questioning the cost-effectiveness of this further development. One would have thought that a 'scientific', non-ideological concern with behavioural objectives would have led at least to the call for a comparison with untidier and more haphazard ways of teaching and checking up. But perhaps it would then be too glaringly obvious that the two approaches counted different things as success.

It should be squarely faced that the objectives approach has serious implications for the freedom of both teachers and pupils, though sometimes in opposed ways. The teacher's freedom is obviously most threatened by the possibility that the selecting of objectives and the testing of their achievement will be taken out of his crude hands and placed in those of the experts. This could happen either under the guise of 'help', or as a direct expression of distrust by administrators. Not only would the result curtail the teacher's freedom, but it would do so very unfairly, since many varying factors affect the degree of success which is possible with a particular group of pupils in a particular set of circumstances.

The freedom of the pupil is threatened principally in respect of self-directed and self-chosen learning. If all learning is to be the outcome of an 'instructional programme', geared to the realization of pre-specified objectives, then there can be no more room for choice, imagination or idiosyncrasy in learning. Furthermore the teacher is put into a position of detailed authoritative direction which may be conceivable, even if it is not desirable, in relation to mathematics and science, but which becomes increasingly misrepresentative of subjects and activities as one moves away from areas of hard fact to areas where different points of view, different perspectives and alternative valuations are both legitimate and interesting.

Like all universal panaceas in education, the objectives approach (one might fairly say the objectives ideology) has some valid limited applicability. If we want to train pupils in certain narrowly defined practical and physical skills, or if we want to check up on their capacity to make correct verbal responses, then the approach has much to be said for it. We shall be able to see how successful and how efficient a training programme has been. But if we have more liberally conceived educational aims, then we shall in many cases still be able to check up on their achievement, but not in terms of pre-specified terminal behaviours. Their expression is behaviourally too diverse, and behaviour is itself too ambiguous, for that to be possible. In some cases unpredictable outcomes turn out to be exactly what we would have hoped for, while in others the full realization of our aims lies beyond the period of schooling anyway.

Such other faults in this approach have been mentioned as that it concentrates on the form in which objectives are to be stated at the expense of giving any guidance on the selection of their content, though form itself could illiberally narrow the content. Even in terms of cost-efficiency, the laborious non-teaching activities involved in this approach are very doubtfully more efficient than getting on with the task and using some admittedly fallible judgment about its success. Important freedoms of both the teacher and the pupil are threatened in the name of a search for efficiency and in the expression of a distrust more characteristic until now of economic rather than of educational relationships. And the means recommended have the dazzle and the hard glitter of a technological rationality which will debunk in importance, or even deny to be real, what its chosen methods are incapable of handling. In the face of such a potential educational disaster, teachers should strive to satisfy their critics that they are still efficiently teaching those basic skills and accomplishments which every mind can see to be important. They may then more reasonably be expected to be trusted to pursue broader educational aims which are less visible and less easily assessed. Failure in the one area could easily create the public resentment to power a politically backed invasion of the other area.

Determining aims by a survey of opinions

So far in our argument, then, it looks as if the determination of aims should be left to the schools, which ought still to be encouraged to go for liberal educational aims and to be warned away from the excesses of the behavioural objectives approach. Any further investigation of aims might therefore seem bound to adopt a statistical survey approach set on ascertaining just what the teachers actually do think. Such a survey approach has indeed been adopted by the Schools Council's *Aims of Primary Education Project*.[3] This project set itself to draw up a list of aims representative of what one might hope to have accomplished with normal children by the end of the primary school. Initially this question was discussed with four hundred teachers, from whom a list of 2,000 aims was obtained. Happily, it proved possible to boil this multitude of obviously overlapping aims down to seventy-two, thus also tacitly acknowledging the very practical point that a good statement of aims must at least be manageable. The boiled-down list was then sent in the form of a questionnaire to some two hundred assorted primary schools, all the teachers in which were invited to score each item for its importance or unimportance. Just over 1,500 replies were obtained.

The replies were duly scrutinized and statistically digested to show which, overall, were considered to be the most important aims. The first eight were as follows: (1) children should be happy, cheerful and well balanced; (2) they should enjoy school work and find satisfaction in their achievements; (3) individuals should be encouraged to develop in their own ways; (4) moral values should be taught as a basis of behaviour; (5) children should be taught to respect property; (6) they should be taught courtesy and good manners; (7) they should be taught to read fluently and accurately; (8) they should read appropriate material with understanding. It is of some interest to note that there was no reference to mathematics, science, the arts, physical education or languages in the eight most important aims. With the exception of reading and moral education, there is a total concentration on attitudes to the exclusion of content.

Various relatively minor points might be made about such a survey approach to the determination of aims. It is reasonable to expect, for example, some discrepancy between what these teachers expressed themselves as being in favour of, and what they actually did. Conversely, what they actually did no doubt set a practical limit to what they were prepared to back as important. Yet again, there might be questions about how representative they were. Plowden found the most successful teachers to be unable to state their aims, yet these teachers suggested 2,000. Does this mean that it depends on whom you ask, or on how you go about asking? Furthermore, one may wonder whether a distinction ought to have been made between what a child of twelve should be.like as a result of all his previous learning, and what specifically should result from the school's contribution, schools being special places with special purposes.

But there are two rather more substantial points to be made about such a survey approach in general. The first can be introduced simply by asking what we are supposed to do with the results. What is their practical force supposed to be? Is it thought that sufficiently complicated statistical manipulation of expressed opinions confers legitimacy, or normative force, on the digested results? Formally, that would be yet another version of the naturalistic fallacy — the fallacy of supposing it valid to deduce value-judgments from bare statements of fact, such as sets of statistics. No such evaluative conclusions could emerge from this survey approach, since at no stage do we hear of the reasons which might have been thought to justify these opinions. It might be the case that a statistical minority of teachers had thought much more deeply, actively and cogently about the question of aims than had the majority, who perhaps were more content just to echo conventional views, yet that minority would be overwhelmed in the process of statistical digestion. Suppose that I, some individual teacher, were at variance with the conclusions of the survey, should I fall into line? Quite apart from doubts about whether the top eight aims themselves form a set internally coherent enough actually to be put into practice, doubts about their wisdom or adequacy might be entirely in place. Majorities do not necessarily have the truth, and if they do it is not just because they are a statistical majority.

The second substantial point about this survey approach concerns the banner of virtue which it flies. This banner of virtue has inscribed upon it the entitlement of teachers to their own opinions about aims, and indeed the entitlement to differ amongst themselves in their opinions. In fact, it is just because teachers have this freedom of opinion that the survey is supposed to be justified, for no-one knows what the teachers think and the survey will find that out. And this might seem to be just the conclusion to which the argument of the previous chapter was tending.

But confusion has been sown here by an ambiguity in the notion of entitlement to form one's own opinion. Of course teachers should be entitled to form their own opinions, but it does not follow that they will therefore do best to rely wholly on their own resources, or that the most that anyone else can legitimately do is wait to see the results. Views formed on aims might be much better if they reflected a considered judgment on the results of someone else's thinking. As Pericles of Athens is reported long ago to have said, while few may be able to originate a policy, all may be able to judge it. A general deficiency of the survey approach in determining aims, then, is that it throws teachers too much on their own resources. Why should they not come to their opinions in dialogue with educationists and others who have given some careful thought to the matter? By comparison with the stimulus to be gained from acquaintance with a developing tradition of inquiry on a question, what we are able to originate out of our own individual resources is likely to be very restricted in scope and limited in its perspective. Surveys of teachers' opinions on aims may have their uses, but they cannot settle what those aims ought, in anyone's considered view, to be.

Preparation for life as an aim

Yet another method for determining aims, and a perennially attractive one, is first to predict the nature of the society into which the children will grow up, then to ascertain what will be necessary to 'fit' them for that society. 'One obvious purpose', said the Plowden Report (para. 494), 'is to fit children for the society into which they will grow up.' Following this approach, the Report then went on to infer from a future of being consumers a need for discrimination, from a future of ever-changing work a need to be adaptable in learning new skills, and from a future of having to live with one's fellows a need for sympathy and understanding. The fact that ten paragraphs later the Report said that children should 'learn to live first and foremost as children and not as future adults', was admittedly an inconsistency, but it need not detain us here.

An obvious difficulty for this approach is that of predicting what future society will be like. Who can foresee the social results of increasing pressure on world food supplies, on industrial raw materials and on territorial space? Who knows what revolutionary scientific and technological discoveries may yet be made? Sir Karl Popper has gone so far as to claim to show that it must be impossible for us to predict the future course of our history.[4] His argument is that the course of history is strongly influenced by the growth of human knowledge. Yet the future growth of that knowledge logically cannot be predicted, since that would imply the contradiction that we already knew what at the same time we were predicting would later be discovered. For example, if I could predict now that in the future it would be discovered how to fuel the motor car on small quantities of sea water, then I would already have to know how that fuelling might be done, and therefore the discovery would already have been made. There is the further difficulty that predictions are themselves new factors in the unfolding chain of events and may themselves stimulate the very action which in the end will falsify them. The practice of outlining scenarios of possible futures is precisely to enable us to act now, while there is yet time, in a way which will modify the actual future. The purpose is not to foretell, from impotent curiosity, the inevitable future course of events.

Nevertheless, Plowden was surely right to assume that some features of our society in ten or twenty years' time can be predicted in broad outline with a reasonable degree of accuracy. Even in the most fanciful flights of science fiction, illustrative of technologies wonderful to behold, many features of human beings remain unchanged, together with the pleasures and problems to which these features give rise. And there are economic limits to the rate at which hardware can change, and political limits to the rate at which institutions can change, assuming that ruin and revolution are both to be avoided. Plowden's predictions therefore do not seem wholly unreasonable.

A further problem in deducing educational requirements from the predicted future of society is that of distinguishing desirable from undesirable futures. The matter cannot be so simple that we need only seek to promote broad trends, for these may be towards unemployment, hooliganism, urban chaos, dishonesty, alcoholism and callous indifference to one's neighbour. A process of selection and rejection must be interposed between the prediction and the aims determined in the light of it. This is to say that educational institutions should be prepared to pass a considered judgment on society, and not simply passively reflect it. A degree of autonomy as against parents and authorities is one necessary condition, though not a sufficient condition of course, of performing that function. The general problem here is clearly visible in Dewey, who on the one hand wished the school to shed its academic isolation and to relate much more closely to 'life', while on the other hand he found much to criticize and dislike in the industrial, social and political arrangements of the 'life' of his time. Perhaps the curriculum should reflect industrial activity, but suppose that that consists of mindless mass production and the total absence of job-satisfaction or of any form of industrial democracy?

With the qualifications in mind that have been made so far, then the aim, or at least one aim, of the school would indeed seem to be to 'prepare them for life'. That seems reasonable enough, on the assumption that children are going to have future lives (an assumption that was often false in Rousseau's time, for example). But a further qualification must now be added. For if this 'preparing for life' becomes so specific as to be a preparation for particular sorts of life, for particular places in the division of labour, or for a particular class or status in the community, then 'fitting' takes on an historically familiar but nevertheless unjustifiable aspect. Now the school would be taking upon itself, explicitly, the roles of selection, grading and placement which the de-schoolers so bitterly attack. If it is not to be an unjustifiable interference with individual freedom, the school's 'preparation' must retain a general character, with corresponding looseness of 'fit'. At the later secondary stage, no doubt, pupils will themselves tend to judge the curriculum more and more by the criterion of relevance to their own chosen futures, and require increasingly greater specificity of preparation. Whether even that should always be encouraged is arguable, though it may be a vain question if co-operation in learning anything else would be refused. But, at the primary stage, the future is more open, and children are as generous and as tolerant as they ever will be towards attempts to evoke their wider interest. The primary school's attitude should therefore be one of widening opportunities, rather than of preparing for particular roles. Society's legitimate future interest in moral behaviour

31

and in making an economic contribution must be related to the individual's claims to having a life of his own and an extended capacity for choice.

Chapter three

Curricular aims and curricular integration

On what might fairly be called the 'traditional' view, the aims of primary education can mainly be stated in terms of knowledge achievements. Correspondingly, there is a curriculum divided into different areas of knowledge called 'subjects', each subject receiving its timetabled allocation of attention according to some customary estimation of its importance. In this way, a primary school child might be called upon in the course of each week to study English, arithmetic (or mathematics), geography, history, nature study (or science), art, craft, music, physical education and religious education. The basis of division into these separate subjects, and indeed the basis for their further subdivision in some cases, is usually as obscure as are the implied estimations of relative importance. But once something becomes traditional, that in itself engenders much confidence in its legitimacy and clothes it with obviousness.

Some criticisms of such a traditional conception of aims are plainly misdirected. This is especially true when such criticism is directed at the supposed vices of formal instruction and of class lessons. For the subject curriculum can be disconnected from these devices. It can indeed be combined with mixed ability classes and with some forms of the integrated day. A classroom in which children are taught individually or in groups may still bear witness to an attachment to the traditional subject curriculum through its spatial organization. Instead of the different subjects being distributed across time by means of a timetable, they are distributed spatially round the room as so many bays, or corners, or designated areas. Alternatively, there might be a looser temporal distribution through subject assignments. But either way the traditional subject curriculum is retained.

Some further criticisms, however, are rather less easily turned. Without entering upon a lengthy digression in each case to estimate the validity of the points made, I shall mention briefly some four such criticisms. The first of these might be to say that the traditional subject divisions are arbitrary. This would be so in the first place because there is no rational basis for the division. The subject curriculum represents an historical accretion which has never been thought out as a systematic whole, though it is fair to say that historical accretions may be discovered on examination to possess a practical wisdom which rationally conceived constructions may lack. But the subject curriculum could be said to be arbitrary in its divisions in the further sense that it does not accord with the spread of children's interests. Those felt interests are in cars, football, the new hamster, pop singers and the like, which interests cut right across any division into subjects. But that, of course, is to assume that felt interests must be our starting point.

A second criticism might be that the aptly called 'explosion in knowledge' has shaken any pretence that the subject curriculum may ever have had to completeness, even to representative completeness. There is so much that is now known and that could be learned that a principle of selection is hard to find, and even the most polymathic of teachers could himself know no more than a tiny fraction of what there is to be known. The growth in publications for school children has now made all this apparent in a way that was concealed, by the necessary reliance on the teacher as a source of knowledge, even as recently as twenty-five years ago. This point has shifted attention to the supposed general skills of 'learning how to learn', which will be discussed in a later chapter.

The aims of the subject curriculum can be attacked in yet a third way. This time it is not the arbitrariness of a division or the incompleteness of representation that is attacked, but the obsolescence of what purports to be knowledge. For much of the value of the knowledge that is sought must be seen in terms of the child's future life as it will be lived fifteen or more years hence, and not just in terms of its present interest. But either what is taught as knowledge will later be seen to be error, or else it will retain its status as knowledge only to lose its social relevance, like the technology of the steam railway locomotive. So rapidly does some of our 'knowledge' become obsolescent that books may be wrong even before their first edition appears. Notoriously this is so with atlases, but even history and mathematics, concerned as they are with the past and with eternal truths, are no more secure. The past does not change, but history is our conception of the past, and that does change, while computer-based technologies make socially relevant a rather different selection from the timeless truths of mathematics. Thus any ideas of 'necessary coverage' are made to seem very short term indeed in their relevance. Nevertheless, it was argued in the previous chapter that there is sufficient predictive basis for finding some 'basic' items of knowledge to be of more permanent value.

Finally, the traditional subject curriculum may be criticized as resting on too narrow a view of aims. For in attaching such importance to the knowledge content of the different subjects, it tends to ignore equally important aims in the spheres of social and emotional development. The children, it might be said, are as isolated from one another and from their emotional life as are the subjects in the timetable. This criticism, however, taken by itself is clearly either a misdirected attack on method once again, or else is just a plea for a further supplementing of what may be admitted to be too narrow a conception of aims.

The child-centred alternative

This 'traditional' conception of aims has what, in its way, is an equally traditional counter in the so-called 'child-centred' or 'progressive' view. To develop the one conception is implicitly to criticize the other. To express the child-centred view in my own way, and in a way which is relevant to the present purpose, I would say that it incorporates what may be called the 'principle of double effect'. For the child-centred theorist has noticed in everything that we do a feature which is of some interest and importance. First, there is the obvious effect which everyone notices in terms of what is sought after or accomplished: the object that is made, the task that is completed, the journey that is done, the option that is chosen, the decision that is made, and so on. But second, and much less commonly noticed in our outward-looking habits of attention, is the reciprocal effect of all this on ourselves. For in attaining or accomplishing anything, at the same time we strengthen or weaken our interest in it, we sharpen or blunt our sensitivities, we form or break habits. Sometimes this has been called, appropriately enough, 'collateral learning'. In the sphere of economic activity it was

35

very much Marx's centre of interest when he studied the effects of capitalism on those who operated it: capitalists and workers alike, for both were seen to be deformed by 'alienation'. Marx was, so to speak, a child-centred economist.

The child-centred conception of aims tends always to concentrate on the second effect of the two that were mentioned: the effect on the child himself of what he learns and what he does. Characteristically, therefore, this conception de-emphasizes the focal subject content of learning in favour of what might be called 'relational' aims, that is, aims to do with how the child is related to his own activity of learning. The child's felt interests, his attitudes and the subjective quality of his experience thus feature prominently, making the phrase *child*-centred rather well chosen in fact, and not just the vague, emotive phrase it is sometimes regarded as being.

The short chapter on aims in the Plowden Report was wholly concerned with such child-centred relational aims at the point where the committee described a 'recognizable philosophy of education' emerging as a quickening trend. These aims could be grouped together into three broad classes. First, there was interest, or confident eagerness to learn, which cuts across all subject divisions. Second, there was the expression of one's individuality, if possible creatively. And third, there was autonomy, or independence and self-directedness in one's learning activities. But we were not told much, at least in that chapter, on what children should be interested in, or should be creative about, or what in particular their autonomous learning powers should be developed in doing. In fact, from here it is only a short step, if a step at all, to such vacuous aims as 'to care', or 'to be aware', or 'to cope', stated without any indication of what it is we are to care about, or to be aware of, or to cope with. And it is no answer at all, or rather a very naïve answer, to state the object here as being 'the environment': *which* environment?

Valuable as this emphasis on relational aims undoubtedly is, it is inadequate as a total conception of aims just because of its silence on content or direction. Yet the child-centred teacher must still have views on this, however implicitly. For how else is he to choose books or to identify directions in which to 'develop' interests? What materials are to be assembled, and what tasks are to be assigned, facilitated or at least made possible? Is there not an important place here for the idea of a balance, or essential spread, of interest and activity, if not each day then at least over a reasonably manageable period of time, such as a week or a fortnight? Certainly in the Schools Council project on aims, referred to earlier, balance was an intuitive idea rated as very important by large numbers of teachers.

But what lies behind the intuition here? And by what formal devices is balance to be secured? It is no real answer to say, as the Gittins Report said in its short paragraph on aims, that 'the primary school should provide for the full social, emotional, moral and physical as well as intellectual development of its pupils'.[1] This is no help if we want to know about curricular balance, since its concern is with a five-sided child and not with a well-balanced curriculum. Each of these five 'sides' could be present in varying degree in any one curricular activity. Thus in doing some mathematics, children may learn to co-operate as a group, learn to enjoy or fear what they do, find the teacher patient and considerate, gain something in manual dexterity, as well as gain some mathematical ideas. The placing last of the intellectual 'side' is curious, too, since this is probably the one out of the five sides which the school is best fitted to do something about, though undeniably it can do something, even if often pitifully little, about the others too.

In practice, a one-sided emphasis on child-centred relational aims to the exclusion of a definite requirement of curricular balance has two results both of which seem undesirable. The first is for a heavy bias towards art and craft work to appear, at the expense of mathematics and even more of science. The second is for activity to converge on existing interests, often with the same activities repeated in different years and without any discernible improvement. This second tendency also witnesses to a curious acceptance by the teacher of the social determinants which have already been at work in forming these interests.

Though in practice it may happen, there is no theoretical necessity why the child-centred conception of aims should lead to these results. If its relevant principle is that of *double* effect, then perhaps attention should be turned again to what children should be objectively accomplishing, as well as how they should be related to such accomplishments. In much the same way, our final criticism of the traditional subject-centred approach was that perhaps it needed supplementing rather than supplanting. It would be surprising if two such long-established conceptions were either of them totally without insight.

And the suggestion that out of their juxtaposition a more comprehensive and adequate conception may be forced to emerge is at least worth exploring.

Four general principles

Let us now try to arrive at some general principles for the primary school in terms of which curricula might be constructed and particular aims or objectives might be selected. No single principle could serve this purpose since it would necessarily have to be very formal and abstract in its nature, with consequently too little to offer by way of practical guidance. On the other hand, such principles as may reasonably be expected will unavoidably have to be general in character. They cannot take into full account the multitude of individual differences between children, schools and their teachers. Nor can they rest upon a comprehensive knowledge of all possible curriculum content, or require accurate predictions of every relevant change in social circumstances. The content for the curriculum legitimately comes from many different sources: from children's and teachers' personal felt interests, from subject specialists who advise or produce textbooks, from a consideration of social needs, from tradition, and so on. I shall assume that there is no shortage of suggestions for the content of learning and I shall dwell instead on principles of selection, derived from the discussions of this and earlier chapters. These principles I put forward in no particular order. They will also bear upon each other in practice, whether by way of being complementary or being in conflict. They may serve as general tests or perspectives for purposes of assessing more detailed proposals originating elsewhere. Hopefully, they may help to provide orientation amongst an often bewildering mass of considerations, and may provide a checklist which shows up an incompleteness or irrelevance in proposals.

A first principle might be simply that of 'preparation for life'. Granted that 'life' is going to be more or less difficult to predict, and granted also that even if it is predictable it still has to be evaluatively assessed, nevertheless certain broad outlines can be projected. Again, the 'life' being prepared for should not be thought of as narrowly confined to paid work, or thought to begin only on finally leaving school. It starts now, and it embraces much both within work-roles and outside them that goes well beyond job skills. In any case, specific occupational destinations cannot justifiably be prejudged at the primary stage. 'Preparation for life', then, may be taken to imply the learning of such knowledge and skills as are relevant to a wide range of occupations and daily situations. It may also be taken to imply the acquisition of a basic moral education, 'basic' in the sense of comprising a relatively uncontroversial core of principles and corresponding virtues, such as considerateness, fairness and honesty. Behind this first principle lie both the legitimate interest of a society in the children growing up in its midst, and also the individual's own long-term best interests so far as these specially concern his relations to others.

A second principle is that of contributing to a balanced general education, 'balanced' in the sense that significant attention is given to each of the several constituents of whatever is included in one's notion of a 'general' education. 'General education' is, of course, the name of nothing very clear. It may simply mean non-specialization within a given curriculum, in which sense sixth-form education usually is not general. It may signify a contrast with specific vocational training, in which case the instruction given in technical colleges would often not be general. Again, it might mean an education suitable for the generality of pupils, unrestricted to any particular social class, sex, race, religion or range of ability. But the sense of 'general' intended here is closer to the traditional concept of a liberal education. And the best contemporary interpretation of that is still P. H. Hirst's,[2] who conceived it as an initiation into some seven or so epistemologically basic 'forms of knowledge'. Of course, differences in ability and in level of intellectual development must importantly modify the force and range of the 'forms' in their curricular bearings, but it is interesting that even many of those who have been critical of Hirst's arguments nevertheless do not wish to reject his conclusions. The various 'forms' (mathematics, natural science, morality, the arts, understanding persons and possibly also religion and at a later stage philosophy) are thought to be justified in various ways. But whether they are thought to be worthwhile in themselves, or are said to be presupposed in any attempt to question them, or are claimed as preconditions of rational choice, or are presented as the backbone of personal autonomy (to list some of the possible justifications on offer), still few people can be found who would be happy with an education which did not even attempt to initiate children as far into these as time and ability permitted. Rival versions of justification are often compatible with unanimity in conclusions, a fact of some importance when a degree of consensus is required.

A third principle is that importance should be attached to the 'relational aims' which have been so emphasized by child-centred theorists, that is to say those aims which are especially concerned with the cultivation or encouragement of certain attitudes. Can what is being suggested as a specific proposal capitalize on children's existing felt interests? Can it help to develop and to elaborate more lasting interests? Does it provide some opportunity for individual choice and expression? Will it help to make children more autonomous, in the sense of being more willing and able to think and act for themselves? There is no necessary conflict, however contingently difficult it may be to avoid it, between the first two principles and this one. In practice, however, some degree of conflict, or at least some need for persuasion and pressure, does seem to be inevitable. The task then is not to capitulate, or to fall into a despair born of highly Romantic versions of children and their natures, but to face such conflicts intelligently, with a steady determination and with an awareness that one's decision or timing may be wrong. This should indeed be so platitudinous as to be not worth saying, though in recent years it has come to seem provocative, even reactionary. Conceivably it may shortly come to be viewed as excitingly original.

Our fourth and final principle derives from the claim made in the first chapter that the school should continue to be conceived as being a special place with special purposes, and should not be regarded as being just a general child-minding institution. Schools are places specially arranged for learning to take place, and under the directive guidance of teachers. In accordance with that conception our last principle would be one of priority, namely that priority should be given to those kinds of learning for which schools are either alone or are best fitted to transmit or engender. Two kinds of learning will stand especially high in such an ordering of priorities: firstly, learning which requires long and systematic development, and secondly, learning which requires for its acquisition teachers who have both professional expertise and good judgment born of experience that has been reflected on. On the whole, these two kinds of learning may in practice be expected largely to overlap. But this priority principle will not sharply divide the pedagogic responsibilities of parents and teachers, nor is it desirable that any principle should do so. But no doubt there will be a reasonably clear division, even if it is not a sharp one.

To summarize, then, we may ask of any suggested curricular proposal, from whatever direction or personal inspiration it may come, the following four questions: Does it provide a useful preparation for subsequent life? Does it provide a worthwhile contribution to achieving a balanced general education? Does it provide opportunities to cultivate educationally important attitudes towards one's learning, over and above the importance of the focal content of the learning? Does it merit a high enough priority to gain a place in that investment of the community's scarce resources called a 'school'? And with these general comments on curricular aims in mind let us next turn to related but subordinate questions of curricular integration.

Curricular integration or differentiation?

A question of curricular organization which has attracted much interest is that of whether the curriculum should be integrated or not. Being integrated, like being open and flexible and ongoing, is very much to be in fashion. And fashions often do some good, if for the wrong reasons, in that it often needs much more than rational argument to shift formed habits and entrenched traditions. Whether such benefits are to be looked for in the present case, however, is something to consider.

The general idea of integration, I take it, always presupposes differentiation. Where nothing has first been differentiated, neither can anything be integrated. There must be separately identifiable elements of some sort which are then brought together and made into a unitary whole. But secondly, the parts are made into such a whole by their subordination to some unifying principle or purpose. They are not just placed side-by-side, as in a heap or pile, like eggs in a basket, like people in a crowd, or like bits of the sciences in 'general' science. The separate identities of the parts have to some degree to be subordinated to a new unifying principle. For example, in an integrated transport system, rail, road, air, water and pipe are seen and managed as complementary components in an overall policy. With racial integration, separate races subordinate their racial identities to a common citizenship and social policy, sharing institutions, jobs and opportunities.

If we turn now to the curriculum, or the programme of learning deliberately selected and arranged by the school, there would thus seem to be three possibilities, and not just two, in organizing what has been selected to be learned:

1 An undifferentiated 'curriculum': just a general learning situation in which nothing is integrated because nothing has first been differentiated out. A free play situation in a generally stimulating environment illustrates this possibility.

2 A differentiated curriculum: different areas of learning are identified and separately attended to, as in the traditional subject curriculum.

3 An integrated curriculum: differentiated areas of learning are now unified in a way which subordinates their separate identities to some common purpose or principle. Sex education provides a good example of this, drawing relevantly as it does on the separate fields of morals, biology, psychology, literature, medicine and no doubt personal experience.

If these are indeed the possibilities then each deserves some fuller comment.

An 'undifferentiated' as opposed to an 'integrated' curriculum is most characteristically found in nursery and infant schools. A general learning situation is arranged without any direction of attention to distinct subject-matters. A wide range of often freely chosen activity is available involving toys, books, materials, pets, apparatus and of course other children. It might be disputed that there is a 'curriculum' at all here, and admittedly we are, so to speak, at the very edges of the concept. Nevertheless, the situation is that of a school and the adult staff are teachers. Selectivity based on educational principles has gone into the construction of the school environment and selection governs the teacher's stimulating or controlling interventions.

The appropriateness of such undifferentiation in the earliest stages is not nowadays seriously disputed by educational theorists. What is much more disputable is how long this approach should last. At least two necessities mean that it must sooner or later be suspended by other arrangements. These are that there is a limit to what can be just 'picked up' in an unconscious way, and that later sorts of learning involve a more systematic progression. (Both of these points will be taken up later in discussing learning how to learn and discovery methods.) When learning has to be more deliberate and progressive than undirected 'picking up' will allow, the teacher then still has the choice between a differentiated, subject approach, or a more integrated approach based perhaps on interests. But whatever outward approach is adopted, the teacher will himself have to think in a differentiated way if he is to know what to choose or to encourage, and how to evaluate success. This is so for the logical reason that if the children's learning is genuinely to be an integration of diverse elements, then at least the teacher must have a differentiated awareness of the diverse elements in order to ensure their presence together. Unsurprisingly, therefore, we find that the Plowden Report, after arguing in favour of an integrated curriculum which avoided separate subject compartments, then went on to discuss the curriculum under eleven distinct 'subject' headings, only sex education being a newcomer to an otherwise very traditional list.

There are alternative forms of differentiated curriculum but no doubt the commonest is that which divides learning into traditional 'subjects': English, arithmetic (or mathematics), geography, history, science (or nature study), art, craft, music, religious education (or instruction, or knowledge) and physical education. Another kind, following the influential ideas of P. H. Hirst, would be a division into various logically distinct (as it is maintained) forms of knowledge or understanding, such as the mathematical, scientific, religious, moral, aesthetic and interpersonal. But if a differentiated curriculum requires not only differentiation in the teacher's head but also in the pupils' awareness too, then that awareness can nevertheless be achieved in a variety of ways.

The most obvious way is no doubt to use a formal timetable, which requires a whole class or group to attend to a given 'subject' for a set time. Alternatively, time can be much freer, though a differentiated curriculum is adhered to, by a division of space instead of time, so that subject 'bays' or 'corners' are arranged around the room or learning area. Within each of these alternative arrangements, the degree of teacher direction can be varied too, from the formal class lesson, through the subject assignment done at a freely chosen time, to an interest or mood-governed selection of differentiated activity within the overall structure. These permutations are important to realize because several (though not all) of the usual criticisms of a differentiated curriculum rest, as was pointed out earlier, on falsely identifying it with formal lessons and a formal timetable. But assignment work and a room divided into bays can be just as much based on a differentiated curriculum. Some at least of the mild hostility behind talk of 'fragmentation', 'pigeon-holing', 'little boxes', 'watertight compartments', 'barriers' and even 'prisons' may therefore be misdirected.

It would seem that some areas of learning (whether they are called 'subjects' is of little consequence) just have to be differentiated within a general learning situation and given specific attention if learning is to be effective and progressive. The language skills of reading and writing require specific instruction and practice however much they are surrounded by a context of interests or topic-relevance, both because undiscoverable conventions are involved and because practice and correction are needed. Mathematics, too, calls for such specific attention. It has fairly strict sequences within a given mathematical topic, even if there is no single unavoidable ordering of topics. Thus if the topic is 'length', a typical sequence might be: practical comparisons of longer and shorter, then the use of arbitrarily chosen units as practical measures, then the standard measures, and finally some formal calculations. Left to chance, mathematical problems will not spin off from other interests in a systematic enough way, whether in the right order, or at the right level of difficulty, or with provision for enough practice, or at the right time. Again, some things have to be given differentiated attention by the children because they call for the use of specialized places or apparatus, or specialist staff. Singing, instrumental music, physical education and French come into this category. 'Integrated' music or physical education is likely simply to disappear. Finally, if the religious conscience clause were to be taken seriously, or to be regularly invoked by children, then religious education would have to be differentiated for moral reasons.

But these several areas — linguistic convention, mathematics, specialisms and religious education — by no means cover the whole of the usual area of curricular learning, and whether the rest should also be given differentiated attention is a much more open question. The curriculum, after all, is a device to be judged as to its best pattern by how well it suits our purposes within the limits of possible variation. If the preference is for orderly structure, with close attention to balance and progression, then a differentiated pattern will doubtless be most in evidence. In that way, teacher-bias and a narrowing drift of interest may be avoided by a system of fairly mechanical reminders built into the organization. But, as a result, the abstraction from 'real life' problems and topics could well be a powerful motivational disincentive to learning, at least with all but the most able. And a closer inspection of the traditional differentiated subjects, and still more their teaching, will usually reveal them to be to some degree themselves already integrations. In music, the children may have to read words and the teacher will offer explanations of the content of songs, or the historical biography of a composer. In history, scale maps will be used, in French songs will be sung, and in geography the historical aspect of location and trade links may be mentioned. For much of the curriculum, differentiation is nothing pure but only a salient emphasis. This much integration, or rather correlation, is usually welcomed by all but the most extreme purist.

As was argued earlier, integration logically presupposes differentiation, the differentiated elements being subordinated to some unitary whole. In what might be called 'loose' integration, the subordination of elements is no more than their selection according to relevance to a topic, theme, or centre of interest. Thus geography, history, science, music and art may be selectively drawn upon for the contribution they can make to some such theme as canals, the sea, railways, flight, India, or whatever. If the theme is the sea, then there may be maps of oceans, the history of voyages of discovery, experiments on floating in salt and fresh water, the painting of scenes beneath the sea, the playing of 'Fingal's Cave', the singing of sea shanties, *Treasure Island* may be read and the economic uses of the sea may be studied. No doubt the justification for such a 'loose' integration of subjects would be that it naturally follows the course of an interest without any arbitrary interruptions or divisions. And a good deal of such general knowledge is acquired in areas where it is difficult to argue that this rather than that must be known, or that this rather than that must be covered. The strongest argument for loose integration is thus motivational. There would be reservations about employing it as an approach to the whole curriculum, however, since arguments were earlier forwarded for thinking that some things should very desirably, even must necessarily, be given at least some differentiated attention. A further reservation must be that 'loose' integration needs to be carefully watched for balance over a period of time, or some of the presupposed differentiated subjects supposedly being drawn upon may be under-represented. A theme such as the Tower of London may draw on several areas, but it is obviously of primarily historical interest.

A tighter form of integration is obtained when elements are drawn upon as contributory to the solution of some problem. In this case we do not just have a variety of things laid side-by-side and drawn together only for their relevance to a common theme. The contributory elements now have a logical bearing by way of being considerations relevant to the solution of the problem. A practical consequence of this is that the pupils as well as the teacher will need to be conscious of the presupposed differentiated elements *as* differentiated, and often as distinct in kind. And just as some studies really have to be given differentiated attention, so too do some other studies have to lead to an integration of this 'tight' kind. Examples would be moral and sex education, political education and technological studies. Lawrence Stenhouse's Humanities Project in some phases of its work with pupils illustrates the same convergence on problems which have logically diverse evidence related to them. At a different level, educational theory is a further example of such integration. No doubt the prime justification for this approach would be its realism, for this is how practical problems come to us and call for solution in real life. But, by the same token, such tasks are complex, and may be more suited to the upper secondary than to the primary stage. At least at first in education we have to simplify to get any grasp at all.

The general conclusion to which this discussion points, then, is that some parts of the curriculum have to be given differentiated attention, while others have to lead to an integration. It is not a case of either/or, as seems often to be supposed. Physical education for practical reasons, mathematics for reasons of sequence, and language skills because of their arbitrary social conventions all have to be differentiated out, at least for some of the time. But moral, political, technological and sex education all necessarily involve an integration of different considerations round some practical or personal theme or problem. And between these two lies a wide curriculum area where choice of approach is more open. This is the area thought of in subject terms as geography and history, science, art and craft, and 'environmental studies' (which means very different things to different people). There is unlikely to be just one right way of proceeding here, valid for all children and teachers in all circumstances, though two wrong ways would be to pursue either approach to the complete neglect of the other. Evaluative biases, very difficult to resolve rationally, will give a characteristic cast to a teacher's approach, this one favouring order, structure, balance and progression, while another's first thoughts, more child-centredly, will be for interest, realism and 'natural' lines of development. In the normal course of things, a pupil passing through a school is fortunate if he meets both sorts of teacher. His concept of human nature is thus enriched as a useful by-product of more focal curricular learning, while his teacher teaches better if he can follow his own dominant nature.

Chapter four

Child-centred education

Child-centredness in primary education is of course nothing new. It is indeed a way of thinking about children and their education which has a very long tradition of theorizing behind it. Some of the classical exponents of the theory would be Rousseau, in his *Emile,* Froebel in his *Education of Man* and Dewey in such books of his as *Democracy and Education* and *Experience and Education.* And if such a list were to give the impression that no British educationists have been prominent in that tradition, then that would be a false impression. One of the most influential was Edmund Holmes, whose little book *What Is and What Might Be* was called by the historian W. H. Armytage 'the manifesto of the English progressives'. Sir Percy Nunn's *Education: Its Data and First Principles* was very sympathetic to child-centred thinking, while A. S. Neill wrote a stream of books full of child-centred remarks and observations. The writings of Susan Isaacs have also been a strong native formative influence.

Child-centred educational theorizing constituted the substance of the literature' of educational reform from the eighteenth century onwards, often revealing differences between one theorist and another but always sharing certain broad themes and principles. At first, this theorizing was particularly directed against the view of children as scaled-down adults whose development consisted only in a quantitative enlargement of their stock of knowledge. Later the attack was directed more against the teacher-centred and subject-centred curricula and methods of the elementary schools. But the most influential recent publication in the child-centred tradition was undoubtedly the Plowden Report. In spite of numerous inconsistencies, doubtless reflecting the diversity of views to be found in most committees, the Plowden Report was not only broadly child-centred in its outlook but it also, as it were, put the seal of official approval on that outlook, with consequent nationwide pressure on the schools to change in the favoured directions. Some of the statements of the Report have already become classic expressions of child-centredness, such as 'at the heart of the educational process lies the child' (para. 9), 'a school is a community in which children learn to live first and foremost as children' (para. 505) and 'the child is the agent of his own learning' (para. 529).

With this long and evolving tradition of educational theory in mind, is it possible to abstract and formulate the essence of it? Can we now command a view of its central principles, loyalty to which marks out an educationist as belonging to this tradition? If there is a single axiom which is the key to this educational theory, then it would seem to be that we should 'start from the child'. Rather than starting from the convenience of the adult world, or from logically ordered subject requirements, or from the future needs of society (or indeed of the child), we should 'start from the child'. With that as the central axiom, we can then proceed to formulate a range of general educational principles constitutive of the ideal educational situation. Equally, however, and starting from the same axiom, we could generate principles for any social institution with bearings on childhood. Child-centredness has implications not only for schools and schooling, but also for parents and family relationships, for juvenile courts and their procedures and decisions, for medical services, and for such material provisions of life generally as clothing, furniture, and the places and objects of children's play. If child-centredness has had less impact in some of these directions than on schooling, especially primary schooling, then various contingencies may account for that but it is out of harmony with the central axiom.

But what exactly is it to 'start from the child'? What does the axiom more determinately imply? Perhaps the first thing that might be said is that it implies a recognition that children have certain rights such as mark them out as persons having their own legitimate and distinctive point of view. The concept of childhood is not just a biological concept implying only the pre-pubertal stage in the development of a human being. Overlying this biological basis is a variety of ways of looking at children. They may be seen by adults as, for example, a form of investment, the returns on which are to be gathered in one's old age. They may be viewed as potential persons who will eventually become actual persons but in the meanwhile should be as quiet and unobtrusive as possible. They may be viewed as a public embodiment of one's un-questionable personal or institutional respectability, appropriately wit-nessed in dress, speech, manners and behaviour generally. They may be seen economically as potential sources of additional family income. But every one of these concepts of childhood involves a view of children in which their reality is deduced from adult requirements. Child-centredness views children as persons in their own right, having pur-poses and interests of their own and requiring scope for a degree of choice and self-determination. Childhood, therefore, is not just a pre-paration for life but a part of life itself, to be taken into account and respected.

'Starting from the child' has also normally been taken to presuppose a certain view of the nature of children, or rather the view that each child has his own uniquely different nature. This individuality is to be respected and no attempt is to be made to mould him into some pre-conceived desirable standard form. Often the respect for individuality has been justified in terms of the child's natural goodness, a property which he has at least until social influence and environment corrupt him in varying degree. 'Let us lay it down as an incontrovertible rule', said Rousseau, 'that the first impulses of nature are always right.' If this doctrine has been more muted since Freud published his findings con-cerning childhood sexuality, it is nevertheless still present. Usually, however, the general claim is now replaced by a list of more particular characteristics which it is reasonable to assume we shall all approve. Thus the child is naturally full of interests and curiosity, and is con-stantly searching for self-expression and to make discoveries. He is self-active and self-developing according to some unique inner principle of growth, and in this connection metaphors are common of plants un-folding their natures in the process of growth. A common generaliza-tion about the presupposed child nature is that the child is an insatiable learner. 'The child is the agent of his own learning,' and Plowden con-tinued, 'Learning is a continuous process from birth. The teacher's task is to provide an environment and opportunities which are sufficiently challenging for children and yet not so difficult as to be outside their reach' (para. 533).

Yet a third aspect of 'starting from the child' is a characteristic psychological picture. To respect the child as a person we must know something of children in general but also something of this child in particular. And this we achieve by a sensitive, sympathetic and imaginative insight into the world of that child's felt experience. It is not enough crudely to observe that a child is dressing a doll, wielding a paintbrush or pounding a piece of clay. How this appears to the child himself has to be imagined. This imaginative and sympathetic insight not only provides the content of what is to be respected, even reverenced, in children, but it is also a principal source of the adult's motivation and satisfaction in the arrangements which he has to provide. The sense of being the privileged witness of a developing mental life is very much part of the dynamic of child-centred practice.

The child's growth as a person is, in a child-centred view, a process which unfolds according to an inner principle, and in a certain sense the child's education is always to be self-education. He is the agent of his own learning and though the teacher's role is vital it is ancillary. This emphasis on the teacher still having an important role is a respect in which the de-schoolers, who in other ways are very child-centred, stand outside the main tradition. The sorts of principle which now follow upon starting from the child are that he should be given wide freedom of choice (though within an arranged environment), that he should be allowed to follow the natural course of his felt interests without arbitrary interruption, that he should learn by discovery rather than from instruction and that he should be allowed a considerable measure of self-expression. At all times the teacher should be mindful that human perfection is doubly relative: it is relative to the unique nature of each individual, with his own pattern of interests and abilities, and it is relative to each stage of that individual's development. As Rousseau said, the standard should be the perfection of childhood rather than an adulthood by comparison with which the child must seem lacking. 'The school should set out', Plowden said, 'deliberately to devise the right environment for children, to allow them to be themselves and to develop in the way and at the pace appropriate to them' (para. 505). It was this emphasis on stage-perfection which raised play to such a level of educational significance for Froebel.

Child-centred theorizing has frequently been silent on the proper principles which are to govern one child's relations with another, the European tradition especially being very individualistic in this respect. It is a positive requirement of Rousseau's that there should be just the one child commanding the ideal tutor's full attention. Other children appear only to play some educationally beneficial part in Emile's carefully structured environment. But the American child-centred tradition, and also the view of such writers as A. S. Neill, is that social relations should be given greater prominence than this. So far as the child's current activities are concerned, the view has generally been that order and rules should be those required by the situation and should be largely self-imposed by the group, who see the point easily because of the natural connection with the situation. Group activities require their own special sorts of order according to the activities which they are and the differing conditions necessary for success. Thus the rules of a game are not some arbitrary outside imposition, but are constitutive of the activity itself and their observance must be wished by anyone concerned to play the game properly. So far as other, usually more general rules are concerned, such as those required for corporate life in an institution, then the principle is that they should be proposed and adopted by democratic procedures. 'The key to all child-centred education', A. S. Neill therefore says, 'is self-government.'[1]

So far as the teacher is concerned, he is certainly not to be a dominating authority figure. His role is primarily to be that of stage-manager. He is to devise the environment and the opportunities for individual growth to achieve its fullest perfection. He is to provide, stimulate, inquire, support, suggest and hint but not to tell, instruct, demonstrate, explain or direct. Above all, he is to be a keen observer, aided by his sympathetic and imaginative insight into the child's world of experience. He is to look for new interests and for signs of a new readiness to be challenged. He must spot growth potentials and then lead them out and provide for their development. The best analogy of his activities is that of the gardener, who can do much to perfect growth if he does it at the right time and in accord with the plant's own natural bent. And all of this calls for a special sort of patience which will not be disturbed by anxiety at an apparent lack of objectively testable achievement. That patience is made possible by his insight into the richness of the child's covert mental life, and his witnessing of the secret inner unfolding.

The tradition thus requires that we 'start from the child'. This is taken to imply respect for him as a person, also a view as to some of his principal characteristics, and a more particular insight into the inner world of experience of each individual child. Such educational principles then follow as that there should be much freedom of choice, many chances to pursue interests, and rich opportunities for discovery and self-expression. And the situation in which all of this takes place should be governed by rules immanent in the activity, or else democratically adopted. The teacher's role is to be a manager of learning-situations, so structuring the environment that the child's self-educative endeavour can most advantageously and naturally proceed to its next unfolding. Such seem to be the broad principles of the child-centred tradition.

Child-centred education considered

'Strong on methods, but weak on aims', is a judgment that has often been expressed on child-centred educational theory. But it may be questioned whether it is possible at all to be strong on methods if one is weak on aims. How could a sequence of activities be regarded as the expression of a method at all if there were no aims, no end-in-view? Is blowing a whistle a good method? Well of course, it all depends on the circumstances and what you are aiming at in those circumstances. Is it to get a train started, or a game stopped, attention in a playground, the boiling of the water advertised, the rescue team directed, or extra help in making the arrest? Blowing a whistle may be a good method of doing all of those things, but we cannot judge that until we know the aim. So if child-centred educational theory is strong on methods it can hardly be weak on aims. Perhaps all that was meant by this epigram was that child-centred teachers can easily get children going on activities, without any motivational problems. But simply to achieve that, without any closer specification of which activities, could be an achievement of little educational value. By all accounts, bedlam is a state of considerable activity.

Then what are the characteristic child-centred aims? Aims there must be, even if they are left implicit and unstated, because choices and decisions constantly have to be made. Materials and equipment have to be selected and ordered, an environment has to be chosen and constructed, and decisions have to be made about the questions one asks and the possible lines of development one sees. In all of these lie value-judgments implying a set of aims. And the characteristic child-centred aims, as I argued in an earlier chapter, are relational rather than prescriptive of content to be learned. They specify the various desirable ways in which the child should be related to what he does and learns, rather than the content of the learning. What he learns is thought to be of less importance than that he should develop good attitudes in learning it. These relational aims can be conveniently grouped under three main headings: (i) intrinsic interest (eagerness, curiosity, learning to learn, absorption, etc.); (ii) self-expression (expressing one's own individuality, being oneself, etc.); (iii) autonomy (making independent judgments, choosing with confidence, self-direction, learning by discovery, etc.). But such relational, or attitudinal, aims leave undeclared the directions in which they will be pursued. As Edmond Holmes resoundingly declared 'let the end of the process of growth be what it may; our business is to grow'. But Hitler grew.

In practice, many child-centred teachers are no doubt more sensible than the pure doctrine might lead one to expect, but to a degree many teachers are also misled by the doctrine (as we can see from several of the firsthand reports in the series of booklets *British Primary Schools To-day*, prepared under the aegis of the Schools Council). Often the necessary value-judgments are there in practice, though disguised in the horticultural language of nourishing or feeding and of not stunting or forcing. But again, plants can be trained to go in different directions, some better than others. Yet one does not really want to depreciate child-centred values as such. To quote from the Plowden Report in a way which reverses the direction of its own concession: 'these are genuine virtues and an education which does not further them is faulty' (para. 506). The relational aims mentioned above are very important. The deficiency of child-centredness, however, is surely to be found in what it neglects rather than in what it celebrates.

Two things especially it neglects, both of them to do with the selection of the content of what is to be learned. First of all, it neglects the importance of achieving a certain balance of spread of activities over a period of time, not necessarily daily, or perhaps even weekly, but within a manageable period over which the teacher can keep steadily in view where the educational process is going. Of course, ideas of all-roundness are often found in child-centred literature. But it is, as we should expect, the all-round child rather than the all-round curriculum which is in mind. The five- or six-sided child is to benefit from an all-round development: emotionally, physically, socially, morally, spiritually and (always last nowadays) intellectually. But what of the kind of all-roundness traditionally celebrated in the concept of a liberal education? That implies an initiation, to whatever degree time and individual ability allow, into a selection of the main forms of knowledge or understanding which have historically developed.

It is none the less true for sounding platitudinous to say that a child has a culture to inherit as well as a self to express. And a selection from that culture made according to the best judgment available ought surely to complement child-centred 'relational' aims. We might even say that the latter can be realized only through the former. In practice, if one scratches a child-centred teacher one usually uncovers the traditional subject curriculum. The Plowden Report in fact proceeded from its child-centred principles to a chapter on the curriculum which was mainly divided into ten very traditional sections. But this does not necessarily mean that virtue triumphs in the end, since the traditional subject curriculum is not necessarily the best conception of a modern liberal education.

The second neglected perspective on content is that of future usefulness, whether for the later stages of education itself or by way of 'preparation for life'. Plowden may say that 'children should live first and foremost as children and not as future adults', but children unavoidably are future adults. It is undoubtedly a great educational and human gain when children are respected as persons in their own right, and childhood is seen as part of life and not just as a preparation for life. But the suggestion here is not that schools should be just a preparation for later life; it is only that that is one important aspect of it. Children still need basic skills if they are to take full advantage of their subsequent education, and it is no service to them, let alone to the wider society in which they will live, if they are unemployable or incapable of social co-operation.

Historically, child-centred theories have usually been wedded to a belief in the natural goodness of children. This is an obscure doctrine, but to the extent that clear sense can be given to it, then it is false. In the first place, it is a fallacy though a popular one to infer from the fact that some characteristic is natural that it is therefore good. What is natural might also be good, but it cannot follow simply from its being natural that therefore it is good. In reality, much that seems to be natural (spontaneous and untaught) would normally be judged to be bad, such as spite, selfishness, aggressiveness, boastfulness and jealousy. These tendencies take their turn along with sympathy, generosity, kindness and other more amiable characteristics. It may have been necessary historically for crude ideas of original sin to be corrected by the contradictory doctrine of natural goodness, but the truth seems to lie somewhere between the two.

Again, the epistemological status of the doctrine is unclear. Is it an empirical generalization? When pressed with apparent counter-examples, a determined advocate of the doctrine, such as A. S. Neill, will retreat until even the foetal environment is blamed for bad tendencies. The fault, he clearly thinks, must be found in some environment or other, and not in the intrinsic nature of the child. The problem of the status of the doctrine is further complicated by the fact that nature is often only too obviously read into the child from whatever unconscious assumptions prevail at the time. Thus Rousseau found it entirely natural for Sophy, destined to be Emile's wife, to have an authoritarian upbringing, to be dependent on the good opinion of others, and to be taught a dogmatic religion. 'Nature', here, is made to bear a face which no women's liberationist would recognize as her own. In contemporary versions, 'nature' is perhaps more apt to look like someone's highly-reflective and articulate niece at play in some middle-class back garden. But whatever the truth of the matter may be, it is evident enough that by school age, even nursery school age, nature has taken on many socially determined characters, some of which are remarkably recalcitrant to any change initiated by the teacher. Language and interests, or their absence, are prominent examples. True or false, 'natural goodness' seems to be an eminently dispensable doctrine.

The relativity of conceptions of 'nature' is sometimes matched by the relativity of the child-centred observer's special insights into the inner world of childhood. The problem of how we can know other minds is a long-standing one in philosophy, though most would agree that we do have such knowledge, however difficult it may be to give an adequate account of its possibility. And it would also be widely agreed that different people have very different degrees of insight into others' minds and experience. There is a world of difference between the one extreme of the person so full of prejudices and self-preoccupations that others appear before him as little more than physical presences, and the other extreme of the person who can immediately read intentions and respond to feelings on the slightest cues and indications. And, since in general ability follows interest, a teacher of child-centred sympathies might be expected to have developed greater perceptiveness and sympathy in this respect. There is no evident reason to doubt that this is often so. But, equally, there is no reason to doubt that many a traditional teacher has, through experience, gained considerable insight into children. But here a caution needs to be sounded. Error is also possible, and is likely to be more frequent if we have a preconceived doctrine as to the nature of the child. For this may lead us to read into children's activities a significance which either is not there at all or else which ought to be set against other features which the doctrine leads one altogether to fail to notice. A reasonably objective and often very rewarding exercise is closely to watch a given child's activities over a period, then to ask the teacher what he thinks the child has been doing. In that teacher's situation, we should probably all be to some degree surprised by the discrepancy, but to the extent that it is doctrinally induced it is not inevitable. Respect for children as persons is not incompatible with respect for truth. It may well be dependent on it.

A further respect in which child-centred views on the nature of children may be questionable concerns the idea of development. Frequently presupposed is an idea of development as an unfolding according to an inner principle. And in physical respects there may be much in this. There may also be much in it to the extent that the development of mind has physiological and especially neurological necessary conditions. It may even be, though doubts have been cast on it, that something very like Piaget's development through distinctive stages is unalterable in its order and not to be hastened in its evolution. But it does not follow from any of this, even if it is all true, that education must be an unfolding. Even Piagetian stages require experience for their emergence. And if we consider the acquisition of objective knowledge, as in mathematics, the sciences and history, then if the truth is to be known belief has to agree with reality and the external discipline of fact is unavoidable. Nor is it just that matters of fact are independent of what we think. The critical standards which have been historically developed in these disciplines also present themselves initially as external, as do moral standards, which would have no point if we did by nature all that morality requires. Getting everything from the child and always starting from an existing interest may therefore be frequently useful practical principles, but cannot be universally appropriate. But in relation to every aspect of children's natures and their development detailed observation, unprejudiced by general doctrinal prescriptions, is really what is most appropriate. That is not to say that we can ever observe without making assumptions, but we can at least be ready to observe on the assumption that we may be wrong in our particular expectations.

In many ways the principal deficiency of child-centred educational theory, where it is deficient, is its failure, or perhaps refusal, to come to terms with the need for adult authority. One is given the overwhelming impression that though teachers may be formally in authority, they should not really exercise that authority in any overt or noticeable way. All can be accomplished in the way of discipline by utilizing the child's own strong interests and purposes, or by appealing to the rules immanent in the playing of a game or the accomplishment of a purpose. And if the reality should stubbornly turn out to be otherwise, then the child concerned is plainly not ready for whatever it is. Doubtless there are instances, education being a highly complex and varied enterprise, where this is indeed so. Nevertheless, justice is still not done to the need for authority, the more so the younger the children.

The fact is that what children do, or do not do, affects their later lives. So too do the experiences which they now have, or miss, involve consequences for their futures. Dewey amongst the traditional child-centred theorists was perhaps the most aware of this. He even tried to extract a value criterion from it. But a child's life now and later is all part of a single life. It is all his life, even though he may now be conscious of nothing beyond to-day or even the present moment. Since he often does not know of his own future, and of the consequences for it of what he does now, he cannot form a judgment of his best interests on any adequate basis. Even his interest in becoming autonomous is subject to this deficiency.

On the frankly paternalistic ground of being in his best interests, it therefore falls to adults who have a special knowledge of him, and a natural or professional care for him, to try to discover those interests and secure their satisfaction on his behalf. Parents and teachers therefore rightly exercise a certain directive influence over him for his good, though to the extent that autonomy is one of his interests then that authority should set itself as one of its tasks its own demise in the face of growing powers of self-direction. This authority is, of course, dependent for its justification on the relevant adult being able and willing to discover the child's best interests, or at least to do so better than can the child himself. Mistakes will no doubt be made, and in the transition period the child will in fact sometimes know better, all of which makes a responsible task that much more difficult. But so far as schooling is concerned, it seems clear that throughout the primary stage general judgments of interest will still have to be made by the teacher and the headteacher. The curriculum cannot simply follow felt interests, but should be liberal in its balance and scope, and it must to some extent prepare for life. Again, true knowledge of fact and the acquisition of the critical standards involved in the discovery of fact are external disciplines which will not always be in perfect harmony with mood and interest. The best accommodation between these sometimes conflicting interests must be judged by the teacher.

Teaching well is a difficult art if only because it requires balancing conflicting claims in order to find the best course in a great variety of circumstances. The individual has claims but he is also part of a group containing others who have equally valid claims on the teacher's limited time. Present interests are sometimes at variance with future needs, of which needs the child himself may even be unaware. Then the tension between the claims of different parts of his own life becomes the tension between the child's freedom and the adult's authority. Eagerness and confidence are sometimes misplaced or misdirected in the light of critical standards and objective fact, so that self-esteem and respect for truth may be in conflict. It is a one-sided simplification in such conflicts to resolve them all by the expedient of always 'starting from the child', just as much as it is an illusion that teaching can ever be an entirely conflict-free, happy and harmonious affair. As well as having a sensitive and sympathetic insight into the world of childhood experience, a teacher also needs determination and a will directed towards the future. It is not too harsh to say that fascinated spectatorial absorption in children and their world sometimes usurps the role of teacher. An essential and valuable source of insight then becomes the object of a form of self-indulgence.

Part two

Teaching and learning

Chapter five

The concept of teaching

There are many problems about teaching, and they are of many different kinds. They reflect the practical difficulties of successfully getting children to learn and of relating to colleagues in reasonable harmony and co-operation. They arise from limitations on one's projects set by time, finance and authority. They may be created by personal uncertainties about one's suitability for the role or one's possible future. But the problem with which I shall be concerned here is a conceptual one. When is someone teaching? Which are the essential features that characterize the activity? And I ask these questions, not from idle curiosity, but because I think that a correct answer helps to shed some light on some otherwise puzzling changes in attitudes towards teaching.

But the question of when someone is teaching scarcely moves us onto virgin ground. Others are already there and with a variety of answers, though some of these answers plainly will not do. B. F. Skinner, for example,[1] characterizes teaching as 'simply the arrangement of contingencies of reinforcement', but this suggestion immediately betrays a pressure to fit, or rather to force, teaching into the scope of a preconceived theory. Not any and every deliberate shaping of behaviour can count as teaching, since not all deliberately induced changes in behaviour are learned. Unsatisfactory in another way is Israel Scheffler's characterization of teaching[2] as requiring us to 'respect the student's intellectual integrity and capacity for independent judgment'. In this account, teaching at its liberal best is equated with all teaching, even that which lays down the earliest groundwork of linguistic conventions, as in the teaching of speech, reading and writing.

A paradigm attempt in the analytic tradition is that of Hirst and

Peters.[3] Their characterization begins from the feature that teaching is an intentional activity, the intention being simply to bring about learning. But even this apparently innocuous start is not without its critics. Some will say that there must be not only an intention but also objective success in bringing about learning. On that view, if you have not been successful, then you have not taught at all. Undoubtedly we do sometimes use the word with that implication in mind, but surely not always. Then 'task' and 'achievement' senses have to be distinguished. Again, there are those who would claim that regardless of any intentions, the simple fact of having learned from someone else is sufficient for a person to be said to have been taught. Thus if I successfully navigate my car through a flood and, unknown to me, someone else observes my progress and learns from it, then I would automatically be said to have taught this unknown observer how to do it. However, if any point of substance at all turns on this issue, then it will probably concern the proper ascription of responsibility. If I 'taught', and what I taught is somehow wrong or undesirable, then I shall be to blame for it. If a teacher's poetry reading has as its regrettable and unintended result that the children hate poetry, then insisting that the teacher 'taught' them to hate poetry is probably just a way of locating a responsibility and so justifying blame.

But even if it were freely granted that teaching is an activity guided by the intention to bring about learning, then still that would not be sufficient to characterize it. Librarians often have that intention, and so too do parents shepherding their offspring through the school gates. They all intend to bring about learning. But the bringing about must clearly be of a more direct nature than that. Middle class financial sacrifices to get a son into Eton might just conceivably be made with the pure intention to bring about learning, but making those sacrifices is not by itself teaching.

Hirst and Peters therefore further add that, in teaching, the teacher must mark out, present, display, indicate or in some way exhibit what is to be learned. This marking out can of course be done in a great variety of ways: by questioning, demonstrating, explaining, instructing, and so on. Necessary too, they say, is an adaptation of what is presented to the learner's level of understanding and to his abilities. To speak to English school children in Russian would not just be a bad way of teaching them, it would not be teaching them at all.

Then do we now have the complete characterization that we sought? Is teaching just an activity guided by the intention to bring about learning, indicative of what is to be learned, and adapted to the learner's present state of understanding and level of ability? There may indeed be circumstances in which that is all that is meant. But a difficulty is that there is a great range of everyday situations in which one person is related to another in just these ways, though we would not naturally speak of the transaction taking place as teaching. Something essential still seems to have been missed out, and it is something the necessary presence of which in teaching does much to explain the negative attitudes towards this activity which have become so evident, especially amongst some of those who like to think of themselves as progressive.

Amongst everyday situations which satisfy the threefold analysis given above would be all of the following: the announcing of arrivals and departures at railway stations and airports; a salesman's demonstration of a wonderful new carpet cleaner; radio news programmes; documentary programmes on antibiotics, Chinese farming or sewage disposal; explaining the way to someone who is lost; showing a neighbour how to change a sparking plug, how to mend a leaking tap or how to prune his roses; and being given advice at a citizens' advice bureau. For in all of these everyday situations, and in very many more, someone intends someone else to learn something, marks it out and presents it to him in a way which is adapted to his level of understanding. But this is still not teaching, and if the message is not learned neither do we have a teaching failure, whatever other sort of unsuccess it may be.

What, then, is the missing element? Why is the station announcer not teaching, whereas the car driving instructor is? Why is learning from a neighbour how to change a sparking plug not teaching, whereas the tutor at an evening class on car maintenance could well be doing that? Of course, it may be said that each of these questions begs the question, though I do not think that that is so. But perhaps a qualification had better be added: the station announcer and the radio newsreader never teach, whereas one's neighbour might do so, depending on how the learning situation was conceived. I do not want to say that teaching, properly so called, occurs only in schools. But typically that is where it does occur, and for the very good reason that a reference to teaching is part of the definition of a school.

The missing element in the everyday situations, I suggest, is quite simply authority. A teacher-pupil relationship, whether in the institu-tionalized setting of a school or outside it, is an authority relationship. That is what has been missed in the analysis previously considered. Of course, many people would be very ready to admit that the teacher must be *an* authority in relation to the pupil. That is to say, the teacher must be more knowledgeable, discriminating, skilled, or understanding than are the pupils on the subject to be learned. You cannot teach something of which you are yourself ignorant. At the very least the teacher must be one page in front of his pupils. The teacher need not be infallible, but if he is too fallible his credibility as a teacher will soon diminish. Yet all of this, though true, is not quite to the point, since it was not authority in this sense that I had in mind as having been missed out.

There is yet a second sense in which authority might be claimed to be necessary for teaching to take place. The teacher, it might be said, must also be *in* authority. His right must be formally recognized to keep order, to direct the movements of pupils, to give or withhold various permissions, to administer punishment should that become necessary, and so on. And in practice all of this is also usually true. De-schoolers bitterly complain about it, on the grounds that it expensively adds a custodial function to the teaching function of the teacher. Teachers may spend a very large part of their time preoccupied by this policing aspect of their job. Theoretically, this function could be kept separate from teaching. It could be performed by someone else who was kept at the teacher's side for disciplinary purposes only, rather like the 'bouncers' employed by clubs and dance halls which have an anarchic clientele. But it is not authority in this sense either that I previously asserted to have been omitted from accounts of teaching. And it is just because discussion of authority in teaching has tended to become polarized between being an authority and being in authority that the kind of authority that I have in mind has been missed.

The missing element is the kind of authority that is exercised in directing the learning process itself. It is analogous to being in authority in that the teacher has to direct, and it is analogous to being an autho-rity in that this direction must be guided by what the teacher knows of the subject-matter and of his pupils. In the light of his knowledge of violin-playing and of the pupil the violin teacher may demonstrate tech-niques, point out difficulties, explain notation, set pieces for practice, critically listen to sample performances, comment on successes and unsuccesses, and so on. The mathematics teacher likewise directs learning according to his knowledge of both subject and pupil. He revises presupposed knowledge, draws attention to patterns, indicates ways of looking at problems and cautions against dangers. He questions and probes, refers back and hints forward. All of this is directive, but it is directive in relation to the developing understanding of the pupil and could not possibly be delegated to some classroom 'bouncer' at his elbow. Nor would such direction be possible without knowledge of the subject, though it requires a knowledge of the pupil as well as of the subject.

The authority necessary to teaching, then, is manifest in such activities as the following: setting tasks, pointing out needs, correcting errors, making critical judgments, identifying dangers and pitfalls, specifying what to do next, directing attention and interest and asking for sample performances. All of this and much more is done by a teacher with a right to do it, and with corresponding role obligations for the pupil. The teacher has the right directively to structure the learning situation, however subtly, intelligently or inconspicuously he may do this. But of course, he has no right to coerce understanding, if such a thing were possible. Here, as elsewhere, authority and power are distinguishable. For there to be understanding, there comes a point at which teaching is always vulnerable to failure, namely the point at which the pupil must effect something for himself: see the relation, master the skill, grasp the point, notice the pattern or come up with the right idea. At that point, too, is presumably to be found the kernel of truth in the contention that all education is self-education. Perhaps it is this kernel of truth which also lies behind Scheffler's assertion that a teacher has to submit what he says to the pupil's rational scrutiny.

This third kind of authority is just what is lacking when the station announcer recites the stations at which the 9 o'clock train will call. It is lacked also by the narrator of the television programme on antibiotics and normally it is lacked too by the neighbour who explains about the roses, or the salesman who demonstrates his new carpet cleaner. They none of them teach, because none of them have the requisite authority to direct our learning. If they should assume this authority, then they would, with unwarranted presumption, overstep certain social limits and in so doing might well evoke resentment, indignation, or even perhaps faint amusement. They would have forgotten their place, which may well allow them to show, tell, explain, inform or demonstrate, but which does not recognize any right to teach. The intended learner may take it or leave it in such cases, or make of it whatever he likes. Of course, if in such a situation we ourselves request to be taught, then the line may be voluntarily crossed, but there is still a line there to be drawn. To learn from teaching is to submit oneself to authority. That is not to say that teachers must be authoritarian, or that this authority must all the time be officiously and assertively exercised, but the authority must be there. Learning from teaching, like all submission to authority, requires a certain humility, which is not the same thing as humiliation. Those who lack all humility will therefore naturally be found amongst the noisiest opponents of the very idea that anyone should presume to teach them anything.

Though teaching goes on elsewhere than in schools, it is intimately connected with the concept school. A school exists where special arrangements have been made for learning to take place under the directive guidance of teachers, teachers being people who have been given the authority to direct the processes of learning. Much learning, even of an advanced and highly systematic kind, may go on in libraries and elsewhere, but such places are not schools if they lack teachers. Schools presuppose teachers, though informal and isolated acts of teaching can occur outside schools. If teaching should vanish from our schools, as some advanced thinkers recommend that it should, then by the same stroke these places would cease to be schools. What would be left might be a very fine resource centre, or recreation ground, or play area, but it would not be a school.

My own view is that teaching deserves, and will continue to deserve, an honourable place amongst the sources of learning. In many primary schools less guilt or discomfiture should be felt at being surprised in the classroom in actually doing some teaching. But perhaps the worst excesses of 'never teach a child anything' will pass once it is recognized that learning is of many rather different kinds and that, while one kind may best be discovered for oneself, other kinds are best learned from a teacher. A substantiation of this contention would, however, require a critique of discovery learning.

Chapter six

Learning how to learn and learning by discovery

The phrase 'learning how to learn' seems to have originated in an article of Harlow's on what he called 'learning sets'.[1] According to Harlow, 'the learning of primary importance to the primates, at least, is the formation of learning sets; it is the *learning how to learn efficiently* in the situations the animal frequently encounters. This learning to learn transforms the organism from a creature that adapts to changing environment by trial and error to one that adapts by seeming hypothesis and insight.'[2] Again, 'it is this *learning how to learn a kind of problem* that we designate by the term *learning-set*.'[3]

But even if the origin of the phrase is indeed to be found in Harlow's article, nevertheless since then it has gained a more widespread currency which seems to owe little beyond the phrase itself to that article. Some more recent quotations will make this clear. For instance, Musgrove writes that 'above all the child must learn how to learn: he must be inducted into subjects which are essentially a way of inquiry rather than a collection of factual information.'[4] Again, Sealey and Gibbon write that 'experience communicated *to* children will be such that, from it, the child develops the ability to perceive structure and so, gradually, acquires the fundamental power to "learn how to learn" which will enable him to think effectively about any subsequent experience in life.'[5] Very recently, Postman and Weingartner have stressed the importance of learning how to learn as a process of improving one's 'unique meaning-making capabilities'.[6] What, according to these authors, is most worth knowing is how to make meanings out of the constantly changing social reality with which one is confronted.

This emphasis on the importance of learning how to learn has also now found its way into official reports on education. Thus the authors of the Plowden Report wrote that 'the child is the agent of his own learning ... facts are best retained ... when children learn to learn.'[7] There is a similar emphasis in the Welsh version of Plowden, the Gittins Report: 'apart from the essential intellectual and social skills of language and mathematics, it seems to us that the child should "learn how to learn", be able to seek information when he needs it, and become increasingly independent of his teachers.'[8] In both of these reports, this advocacy is coupled with the advocacy of developing in children the child-centred value of autonomy.

A universal skill?

How is learning how to learn different from learning how to ride a bicycle, make a dovetail joint, or use a telephone? In both cases, there is a 'learning how to' which suggests some skill as the object of the learning. But 'learning how to learn' is not specific in the way that learning such skills as how to ride a bicycle are specific. Learning how to learn is at one stage further removed from any direct specific content of learning. It might therefore reasonably be called 'second-order' learning. There could be many such comparably second-order activities, such as deliberating how to deliberate, investigating how to investigate, thinking out how to think things out, and so on.

Then is 'learning how to learn' a super-powerful unitary skill employable in all first-order learning whatsoever? Indeed if it were a piece of learning which would really enable us to 'think effectively about any subsequent experience in life', then here would surely be the modern answer to Spencer's question about what knowledge is of most worth. But that it could be such a super-powerful unitary skill or strategy seems very unlikely as soon as one reflects on the enormously divergent variety of first-order learning. What it would be much more plausible to contend would be that learning how to learn marks out, not a unitary skill, but a family of structures of second-order learning having *wide* first-order application. Thus there would be different kinds of learning how to learn related to different general classes of more specific learning tasks.

Certainly this interpretation permits a readily comprehensible application to the notion. In fact, even babies could be said to learn how to learn more specific things, as when they learn to carry everything to their mouths, or to manipulate things, or to incline their heads so that they can look at particular new sources of noise. Later still, young children learn to ask adults for information and help as a way of learning more specific things that they wish to know. In fact, even the very traditional classroom, with its predominantly formal methods of class teaching, required that children should learn a corresponding skill of how to learn. Learning how to learn in that situation was a matter of learning to listen, to attend to what the teacher said, to control one's phantasies and wandering thoughts and to ignore external distractions. Learning how to learn was indeed present there, but it took the form of learning how to concentrate intelligently and attentively on what the teacher said by way of didactic instruction. In this way, students have to learn how to learn from lectures, tutorials and seminar discussions. Recent research into methods of teaching in higher education has made lecturers rather more conscious of this fact.

The point of drawing attention to these applications of the notion of learning how to learn is certainly not to show that there is no new thing under the sun. It is rather to show that the recent emphasis, illustrated by quotation at the beginning, can only be an emphasis on one new *sort* of learning how to learn, not a new emphasis on it absolutely. And the sort of learning how to learn in question is learning how to learn for oneself, independently of the teacher. The switch here is quite comparable to the historical switch of emphasis to experience and activity in educational methods. For all educational arrangements involve some sort of experience and activity, even if it is only that of sitting still and listening. But in this case too there was a shift in what was stressed, and not an absolute innovation. The shift was towards practical and concrete experience, and towards physical and manipulative activity.

The recent emphasis on learning how to learn, then, is neither absolutely new, nor does it imply the discovery of a single super-powerful skill of absolutely universal application. On the contrary, the term picks out a class of skills or strategies having in common only that they are of more or less wide application in facilitating relatively more specific sequences of learning. The relevant class is of such skills or strategies as a child might independently employ in learning, as opposed to the more traditional general skills and strategies for learning directly from teachers. And it is this connection with independent activity which makes the connection with autonomy that is of interest to child-centred theorists.

However, closer inspection of some of the recent advocacy of learning how to learn reveals that it is not just one type of skill or strategy that its advocates have in mind. Different writers have at least five rather different things in mind, which have not commonly been distinguished. First of all, there is learning how to get information on a given topic. The skills involved here mainly include knowing how to use libraries, for example how to exploit classifications, contents lists and indexes, reference books and atlases. Of course, such learning is limited by the reader's capacity to understand what he reads and by the ideas that it will occur to him to pursue. Plainly there is a danger of mere verbalistic copying of material from the books consulted. Often a topic will be suggested by browsing amongst given books, rather than being pre-chosen and used as a criterion of relevance in going to books. But, within limits, and especially at an earlier and less systematic stage of primary schooling, this sort of learning how to learn does seem to be valuable. It appears to be what the Gittins Report had in mind.

A second possible meaning of learning how to learn would emphasize the learning of general rules and principles which can be applied to the solution of a wide range of more particular problems. An elementary example of this would be using a phonic approach to the teaching of reading, where each phonic rule serves for decoding a corresponding whole class of unfamiliar new words. Scientific and moral principles of a general character could be seen as serving a similar function. For instance, the principle of the electrical circuit can be applied in solving a variety of problems concerning switches, wiring patterns, testing to find conductive materials, and so on. Moral principles can similarly be applied in coming to a more adequate and considered judgment on particular actions or rules. This sort of learning how to learn is, however, not new, and so cannot be distinctively illustrated from contemporary thinking.

A third and currently much emphasized species of learning how to learn concerns the 'logic' of different forms of inquiry. Here what is required is that, instead of applying his mind to learning a mass of particular findings in a given subject, the learner should master the methods of inquiry which have produced those findings. He should learn the sorts of questions which can be asked, and the criteria by which different claims can be validated or their particular content verified. In mathematics, for example, the learner has to learn the axioms of arithmetical or geometrical reasoning, and the transformations which count as valid. Concrete analogues may facilitate coming to such an understanding, especially in the early stages. The logic of scientific inquiry has similarly to be learned, including the decisive role of observation and the importance of experimental control over known variables in a situation. Again, with historical or social studies, the sorts of questions which can profitably or sensibly be asked, the moves which count as valid and the checks which need to be made are what have to be learned. Of course, a full understanding of such principles of inquiry could not be gained quite apart from going through any particular inquiries, but the emphasis and results of such an approach would be very different from a more traditional fact-memorizing approach. The pupil would not simply have learned this and that, but would have learned how to learn in that particular field. This type of learning how to learn is an important bridge between child-centred attitudinal aims and the aim of giving a general education.

Yet a fourth meaning concerns what might be called the self-management of one's learning activities. The object here would be to learn how to exploit one's capacities to greatest advantage in learning. It would include, for example, retention strategies such as spacing practice, seeking structural meaning and summarizing in one's own words. Heuristic strategies could be included, such as taking care that one had clearly perceived the problem, checking that one's assumptions were safe, breaking the problem into parts, using diagrams, sleeping on problems. Also included would be learning how to organize one's time and to use one's effort most economically and advantageously. This species of learning how to learn has fullest application at the advanced student level, but it does have some application at every stage of formal schooling.

A fifth and final meaning which can be culled from recent thinking would more perspicuously be called, and often is in fact called, simply 'learning to learn'. For what is learned here is not so much how to do something as an habitual disposition to do it. 'Learning to learn' in this sense is analogous to learning to behave, learning to avoid the rush hour, or learning to enjoy music. Learning is itself something which one learns to do, as being perhaps intrinsically rewarding. Where this is stressed, as in the Plowden Report, then such motivations as the satisfaction of curiosity, the enjoyment of discovery and of problem-solving, the excitement of new ideas, and the gaining of a sense of mastery will be highly regarded. But though a connection can easily be made between this and learning *how* to learn, strictly speaking it is something different, and in that case we have really distinguished four senses, and not five, of 'learning how to learn'. To summarize, these might be called: (i) information-finding skills; (ii) general substantive principles; (iii) formal principles of inquiry; (iv) self-management skills. We are now in a position to make some general observations about learning how to learn, and to consider its links with autonomy.

Learning how to learn and autonomy

A person is autonomous to the degree that he shows initiative in making independent judgments related both to thought and to action. His actions stem from and execute his own plans and deliberations. Now if this is so, then clearly learning how to learn in its various senses will be of great value in aiming to develop autonomy in children. For to the extent that they become capable of learning for themselves, and exercise that capacity, to that extent what they learn is determined by themselves. There are, however, some general observations which need to be made on this preliminary remark.

Making learning how to learn an objective does not dispense with the need for teaching. At the very most, it shifts the content of what is taught from particularities to the skills, principles and methods of general application which constitute having learned how to learn. Furthermore, this shifting of the object of teaching from first-order content to the second-order equipment of autonomous finding out involves rather more than just teaching what these second-order skills and strategies are. It involves training and practice in their use, with accompanying habits of persistence, patience, tolerance of frustration, delaying gratification and concentration. Neglect of this executive aspect of the new emphasis results in disappointments and unjust inequalities. Teachers who make the transition to the new classroom regime without regard to the need for support and plain pressure are likely to be disappointed. And children coming from homes where no habits in harmony with these new arrangements have ever been developed will be at a disadvantage by comparison with children from homes where habit-training and analytic language modes have already created a readiness for what the school can more systematically offer.

Again, however successful a teacher may be in training children to learn for themselves, there will remain much of a first-order character which, for reasons of empirical necessity, still has to be directly taught. This may simply be for greater efficiency in the limited period of schooling available, or because failure, muddle and confusion have resulted from self-directed learning, or because consolidation and practice of past learning are now needed. Self-styled progressive teachers and educationists seem now to be recognizing, with the air of bold admission, that such a degree of direct first-order teaching is still necessary. And to the extent that this is so, as also to the extent that the skills of learning how to learn have themselves to be taught, then learning how to learn in the more traditional uncelebrated sense will still have a place, i.e. learning how to learn from a teacher, by attention, listening, setting aside distractions and so on.

One way in which a connection can be seen, then, between learning how to learn and autonomy is that the former is justified as an educational policy by its value for the latter. Learning how to learn is a means to the development of autonomy, and it is so not just contingently, through some causal connection which might have been otherwise, but logically, through being already a partial instantiation and progressive realization of autonomy.[9] A secondary, though very important, justification of learning how to learn in the classroom is of a more clearly instrumental kind. For once a child has achieved, through teaching and training, a measure of self-direction of this sort, then he becomes less teacher-demanding in his activities. This is very valuable in a class of mixed ability, or in a class organized along the lines of the 'integrated day', because in those circumstances it is a difficult organizational problem for the teacher to divide his teaching time adequately and fairly between several groups or individuals. A further gain is that the impossibly polymathic demands on the teacher's knowledge are eased, especially through the training in the information-getting skills referred to earlier. What a teacher need not be expected to know he may yet be expected to know how to find out.

The current emphasis on learning how to learn has yet another important aspect, so far not touched upon. This relates to what Postman and Weingartner identify as the most striking feature of modern, developed societies: constant change, both technological and social. One aspect of this is that everyone is likely to have to change his job, or to change in his job, not just once but several times in his lifetime. Life has become a process of continuous re-learning. It has virtually ceased to be possible to learn anything in a way which will be permanently valid or valuable. This has dizzying implications for schooling in its aspect of 'preparation for life', since the 'life' which will actually be lived is in many respects unforeseeable. Specific vocational training is likely to be for a job that has changed or even disappeared by the time that the training is completed. In these circumstances of Heraclitean flux, the notion of learning how to learn has found powerful favour as offering something that can be taught of more permanent value. At this level of second-order learning, a stability may be found which is only chimerical at any first-order level.

But this situation can induce a curiously misconceived relativism. This is well illustrated in the work of Bloom[10] when he says: 'we recognize the point of view that truth and knowledge are only relative and that there are no hard and fast truths which exist for all time and all places.' But surely, if a fully specified proposition 'p' is true, then it is part of our concept of truth that 'p' is true for all times and all places (though not of course *of* all times or *of* all places, e.g. Bonn can truly be said to be the capital city only of West Germany, and only since the Second World War). It is not that the world *was* flat and now *is* round; rather it is opinions about the world's shape which have changed, from false to true opinions no doubt we would say.

There are, however, acceptable senses in which knowledge can be regarded as relative. Certainly something can be known at one time or place, and not at another, or to one social group and not to another. But these are really sociological points about the distribution of knowledge rather than logical points about the knowledge-status of what is believed. Again, certainly something *thought* to be true at one time can be refuted or corrected at another. Thus we now think that the world is round (or very slightly pear-shaped, in fact), and we now think that we have a more adequate understanding of the atom, the nervous system and mental illness.

Often of course, it is not so much that some piece or field of supposed knowledge is refuted or corrected as that it is discarded as useless. The technology of the steam railway locomotive is not falsified by the introduction of diesel or electric traction, but simply set aside and forgotten as being no longer relevant to social and economic needs. Furthermore, no more permanent value could be found in learning how to learn if the particular things then learned were not in fact true, or at least a fair approximation to truth. Valuing learning how to learn for its many changing and more particular employments would then be incoherent.

But these misconceptions about relativism aside, it is clearly the case that much that we learn is later discredited, discarded or improved upon. There is a large element of obsolescence in what we learn of a more particular kind. Road systems, public transport timetables, locations of offices, addresses of people — all are likely to be changed in a short period of time, and often even by the next time that we want them. Jobs change in their requirements almost daily, often suddenly disappearing altogether.

A new twist is thus given to Spinoza's perception that autonomy makes us less the creature of fortune. For if learning how to learn equips us to cope with change by helping us more efficiently to re-learn our jobs, or to re-orientate ourselves in changed circumstances, or to learn new jobs, then to that degree we are less at the mercy of fortune and more the determiners of our fates. It is worth adding, however, that in curriculum terms this new emphasis has rather more validity in relation to mathematics and the sciences than it has for the arts. One's enjoyment of Jane Austen, Tennyson, Rembrandt, or Beethoven is not suddenly made redundant, or invalidated. New interpretations of works of art cannot destroy the fact of one's actual enjoyment in the light of understanding one already does have. But the notion of learning how to learn nevertheless has applications here too, in relation to how we can find our way into an appreciation of a new work or form of art.

In one way, however, this aspect of the importance of learning how to learn would militate against autonomy. For Postman and others tacitly concede all the initiatives to socio-economic-technological change. As individuals, it is tacitly assumed that all we can do is respond more or less adaptively and self-directedly to these external changes. This obviously detracts from personal autonomy in that much in our lives is then conceded to be properly externally determined at least in its occasion and pressure on us. This, however, perhaps under-estimates schooling as also being to an extent an end in itself, and not just a preparation for some future of kaleidoscopic change. It under-estimates educational institutions as being to an extent themselves autonomous institutions in a society. At this point, however, developing autonomy as an aim passes beyond simply equipping people with a capacity to learn how to learn. It points to the necessity of having some sociological and perhaps also political awareness of the social process, and having a value-perspective on that. It may well point to a rather special significance of social studies for the development of autonomy.

Learning by discovery

Closely related both to the development of autonomy and to learning how to learn is the notion of learning by discovery. In fact learning how to learn and learning by discovery are not always distinguished in current educational literature. But distinguished they should be, though it can be conceded at once that there is some overlap between the two notions, both in content and in background concerns. The present chapter will therefore be concluded with some discussion of learning by discovery.

So often with educational ideas, to go for the word is to miss the substance. Usually, the word gives only the vaguest indication of what all the fuss is about. Who, for example, could ever guess, simply from a good knowledge of the English language, what the 'integrated day' was? If 'discovery' is taken literally, then it would be a very simple matter to show that children have always discovered things, and that there is no subject or activity that is not full of possible discoveries for children to make. Children discover where it is warmest in the classroom, how Mr Jones reacts to noise, what happens if you mix red and blue powder paints, what sounds different objects make, when the class has a tele-vision lesson, and so on.

All of this is discovery, but not much of it is to the point: the substance has been missed by concentrating attention on the word. Nevertheless, it is not by mere chance or accident that the label 'discovery' has become attached to the new emphasis in learning which the fuss really is about. The ordinary meaning of the term is not irrelevant. And so in learning by discovery we may reasonably expect children to learn something new: to them, at least, if not to the teacher or in relation to human knowledge generally. We may also reasonably expect children learning in this way to do so through some initiative of their own. But to go much beyond that means looking at the actual pre-occupations of the educational debate, and not just scrutinizing a word.

Three things in that debate strike me at once. First, it is primarily the learning of facts, concepts and principles which is at issue, not usually the learning of skills, techniques or sensitivities. In curriculum terms, the subjects and activities of most relevance to discovery learning seem to be mathematics, science and studies of the local environment. 'Creativity' is the corresponding preoccupation in most other areas of the curriculum. Second, a broad and obvious contrast is drawn in the debate between learning from direct teaching, whether from instruction, demonstration or explanation, and learning through a more self-active mode of mental operation, such as achieving an insight on one's own, or through a personal initiative in finding out. Often, this insight or finding out is to stem from some concrete and practical experience, but it may also result from going to books. Finally, this learning by discovery is not envisaged as something that typically just happens. It is designed to happen, as a result of a definite teaching method or strategy. At least five different strategies can be distinguished, which it may be useful at this stage to describe.

Type A

For the most part, the teacher is a mute presence. His task is to 'structure the environment', or to provide 'structured apparatus'. The children are then to learn the relevant facts, or are to abstract the relevant concept or principle, in the course of self-chosen activities. The 'method' consists of providing and arranging suitably enticing materials. For example, through playing with a blob of plasticine the conservation of volume is to be discovered. Through investigating a tray of assorted materials and magnets, facts about magnetism are to be discovered.

Type B

This is broadly similar to Type A, except that the teacher supplements the self-chosen activity with her own seemingly casual commentary on it. She asks questions about what is being done, supplies information, suggests further activities, and draws attention to certain features. Visits to building sites, museums, farms, waterways and churches well illustrate this form of learning by discovery.

Type C

This is principally concerned with books or, more broadly, with textual resources. Through referring to these resources, a wide range of facts may be discovered. Those anxious to give grand names to simple things may speak here of 'research', daring anyone to contradict. For example, if the topic is 'tea' then books will be consulted, the Indian Embassy may be written to, Assam will be discovered in an atlas, and so on.

Type D

With this variation, a task is set or proposed by the teacher. But the task requires independent activity for its completion. How it may be completed is left open, and the sort of result to expect is not very precisely indicated. 'See how far back a ball bounces from different heights. Try different sorts of ball and different heights.' 'Look for a quick way of adding up all the whole numbers from 1 to any given number.' The now familiar traffic census could be another example.

Type E

This final type might be called 'Socratic questioning', after the episode with the slave boy in Plato's dialogue the *Meno*. The teacher hints, provokes, asks leading questions, confronts the learner with the implications of what he thinks, or prods him into framing some hypothesis. The object is to stimulate active, searching thinking in some specific direction, but always to stop short of actually telling anything. An illustration would be an exchange with a group of children leading up to the formulation of a definite hypothesis about where plants extend themselves in growing.

These, then, are five strategies for stimulating learning by discovery that I have come across. Some of them overlap or differ only in emphasis, of course. And there may well be other types that I have missed altogether. But there are, I think, sufficient examples and types here for us now to attempt a critical assessment of learning by discovery.

A general but very important question to begin by asking is What things could, at least in principle, be genuinely discovered by children? It seems clear that there is much in any ordinary curriculum which certainly could be discovered, but not everything. For instance, it is not possible to achieve an insight into something that is true only by convention, such as the gender of French nouns, or the English system of weights and measures. Again, an upper junior should be able to work out for himself the spelling of a strange word such as 'compensation', but not the spelling of 'manoeuvre', because it follows no rule that he could have inferred. With structured apparatus, such as Cuisenaire rods, it is possible to discover such facts as that two yellows are the same length as one orange, but not the conventions as to what layouts and placings will represent the operations of addition, multiplication, and so on. Such conventions are best straightforwardly taught. This limitation set by conventional truths shows the doctrinaire absurdity of the maxim 'never tell a child anything'.

Another doubt that I have about what could be discovered is much more important but very hard to present sharply. It particularly concerns Type A discovery from a 'structured environment', and also Type B if it is carried on for too long. The validity of these approaches is no doubt best seen in a good nursery, infant or first school, where children can and do discover an immense amount from a fairly free exploration of a carefully designed physical environment, or from a well-chosen outside visit. They discover how balls rebound, how people react, their own physical powers, the properties of sand, water and dough, how to get the toy that they want, what lives round the edges of a pond and so on. All of this is very important, but it is in a sense superficial: it lies on the surface of things, open to natural curiosity. My doubt concerns whether such more-developed and differentiated forms of understanding as mathematics and science could be learned in quite the same open-eyed way.

What the teacher may see as 'structured' in a particular way can always be seen (and used) in very many other ways. How can the teacher's seeing it as structured in that way guarantee by itself that children will see it in just the same way? It is just as open to them to assimilate it to already familiar concepts and uses, which will be misuses only in relation to the teacher's intentions. For instance, there is a wealth of mathematics to be seen in the fifty-pence piece — if you are familiar with Reuleaux curves. Otherwise it is just the queer-shaped coin. Certainly 'mathematics is all around us', but you need more than eyes and natural curiosity to see it.

Forms of understanding such as mathematics and science are cultural achievements. Their insights have been historically accumulated and have often needed genius to attain. All of this cannot be rediscovered by a confrontation with objects, no matter how carefully structured or expensively produced they are, or how actively they are manipulated. If discoveries are to be made here, and many can be, then they must be made by a limited reaching forward from within a growing understanding of these ways of thinking. They require the definite guidance of articulate teachers, or teacher-substitutes and teacher-extensions such as television or work-cards. And this in turn presupposes that the teacher will himself be sufficiently familiar with these forms of understanding. Without that familiarity, how is he to ask opportune and fruitful questions, or even to recognize when a genuine discovery has been made?

Discoveries do have to be discoveries, and not just exciting errors, muddles, confusions or blankness. There is an objective side to making a discovery, as well as the subjective satisfaction. Only ironically can a child be said to have 'discovered' that heavy things sink. (How about an aircraft-carrier or an oil tanker?) Respect for truth is involved here, as well as personal satisfaction. Again, external discipline may meet with impatience and frustration, as well as enjoyment and success. An opportunity to discover is also an opportunity to fail to discover, which is likely to make learning by discovery slower and less certain than learning from intelligent instruction and explanation. In this, as in everything, children will no doubt come to school very differently prepared by their home backgrounds in terms of curiosity, general knowledge, acceptance of an independent role, and familiarity with analytic modes of thought and talk.

Everything in education always has its drawbacks. Therefore having some is never by itself a knock-down argument against anything. Where discovery learning is concerned, we should now ask what possible merits might outweigh those drawbacks. Some say that retention of what is learned will be much better, and also that 'heuristic strategies' of more general value will be learnt. But there is no clear evidence to favour either of these two contentions, and neither seems obviously likely to be true.

The Plowden Report's strong backing for discovery methods is in terms of the Piagetian doctrine that 'the child is the agent of his own learning'. What that doctrine means, I take it, is that each child actively constructs his own mind through a process of interaction with his environment. Certainly the spontaneous construction of reality in babies is deeply impressive. But the truth of the Piagetian doctrine cannot be used to justify preferring learning by discovery to learning from instruction, because the doctrine is compatible with *both* ways of learning. The learner just interacts with something different in each case.

Learning language is an actively constructive process, often displaying intelligent mistakes ('I maked', 'he holded', 'mouses'). But, as a set of conventions, it is not learned by discovery from things. Parents instruct children in 'what we say' and provide speech models for imitation. The 'agent of his own learning' actively makes sense out of that direct teaching. Instruction, intelligently adapted to the learner and coupled where appropriate with suitable concrete and practical experiences, could also satisfy the Piagetian doctrine. It *must* satisfy it, since children do in fact often learn in that way.

Perhaps the distinctive merits of learning by discovery are to be found by looking for different sorts of objectives, rather than in arguing over comparative efficiency in achieving the same objectives. The characteristic objective of instruction is that a certain amount of knowledge should be passed on and learned. Remembered content is the criterion of success. Learning by discovery is more concerned with attitudes, even if that difference is never absolute but only one of emphasis. Learning by discovery characteristically aims to engender intrinsic interest, both in what is learned and in the process of learning it. It also emphasizes the satisfactions of learning independently. But the development of both intrinsic interest and independence in learning are extremely important liberal educational aims. If a method in the hands of some teacher is successful in achieving these aims, then it has much to be said for it, at least as one valid method amongst others.

Chapter seven

What is the integrated day?

The concept of the integrated day is in certain respects like that of the permissive society. Each is felt to be amongst us and to be increasingly prevalent. Each tends to arouse passions and to cause people to take sides. And in the case of neither is there an authoritative original doctrine which can be pointed to, and to which anyone irritated by vagueness might go with relief for an account of the 'real meaning' of the term. This being so there may be some merit in pausing before rushing to express opinions, and in trying to give a little more definition to the concept. But definition is not much help if it is arbitrary, no matter how precise it is, so the attempt at definition made here is made very much with an eye on the actual practice of those who already regard their days as integrated. Some little help may also be gained from the literature on the subject, which can in fact comfortably be read in the space of one evening.

A conceptual map

It would seem a good plan in defining the integrated day to show its place in relation to certain other concepts of great structural importance in understanding a school. I want to begin therefore by making myself a simple conceptual map on which to locate the integrated day in relation to other things.

A school, I take it, is an institution, the distinctive purpose of which is that people should learn things under the formal guidance and control of teachers. Schools may also feed, medically care for, create happy atmospheres, foster satisfying personal relationships and so on, but so also may other institutions. Important as these things may be in a school – and clearly the right sort of personal relationships between teachers, children and parents are crucially important — it is nevertheless the activities of learning and teaching which point to the distinctive intentions behind the provision of schools. Nor need this learning be narrowly conceived. It may embrace facts, skills, attitudes, interests, awareness, appreciations, habits, virtues and the understanding of concepts, or some selection of these and perhaps other things too. All this seems to be true whether we are considering grammar or driving schools, riding schools or Sunday schools, the schools of a university, or indeed the primary and secondary schools to which the great majority of our children go.

But to form a clearer picture of the learning and teaching activities of a school we need to have some answers to our queries on at least four main points: aims, curriculum, methods and organization. By 'aims' here are meant the learning outcomes which the teachers think valuable. By 'curriculum' is meant the varied programme of activities by which it is hoped to achieve those outcomes. If, for instance, fluency in speaking French becomes a new aim of the school, then curricular innovations must obviously follow. Some broad programme of activities must be developed to achieve the new aim. By 'methods' are meant the general and specific ways in which particular curriculum activities are guided and controlled. The 'teaching' here may be indirect as well as direct, since to a varying extent it may be necessary for children to learn how to learn things for themselves. So-called discovery methods are an example of such a recent innovation. Finally, there is the 'organization' of the learning and teaching in a school. This heading covers the ways in which the sequence of activities is changed in the course of the day, and the ways in which the children are grouped and regrouped, and the teachers attach themselves to various groups or classes for different purposes. Family grouping is a recent example, at least in urban schools, of a primarily organizational innovation. Of course, all four of these major points about a school are closely interrelated. If any one of them has logical priority over any other then surely it will be aims, though even aims cannot be settled apart from a knowledge of the children to be taught and of the society of which the school is a part.

Where on this conceptual map could integration plausibly be located? That is to say, where could we look for a sensible putting together of things into a whole instead of a differentiating and separating out into parts? We could hardly start by integrating methods, since these will be greatly dependent on the nature of the curriculum. Again, aims could hardly be sensibly integrated, since being educated is such a complex and many-sided achievement that it must have many aims. We might however, and often do, pursue several aims at once by means of an integrated curriculum. Instead of having a programme of activities formally differentiated into separate kinds of learning, as with the traditional subject division of the curriculum, we might instead have a sequence of activity serving now this and now that aspect of our aims. Something like this is what we have with projects, environmental studies, centres of interest, visits and play. At the secondary level a typical curriculum integration uses the humanities, i.e. English, religious education, geography and history, while mathematics and science are often still pursued as differentiated activities.

Finally integration is clearly applicable under the heading of organization. For instance when children are undifferentiated by age, then there is vertical or family grouping. When children are undifferentiated by ability, then there is nonstreaming. Both vertical grouping and nonstreaming are forms of organizational integration. Again, team teaching integrates separate classes into a single teaching unit. Other possible sorts of organizational integration might relate to handicapped children, racial groups and different social classes.

The integrated day located

Where then is the integrated day to be located on this map? Since a day is a unit of time, then the integrated day must be an organizational concept and not, at least in the first instance, a concept to do with aims, curriculum or methods of teaching. And indeed across all the many varied conceptions of what an integrated day is, there runs the common and unifying thread that set timetables, or other formalized ways of changing from one activity to another, are abandoned. Instead, the flow of children's learning activities is broken and changed informally and often individually, with a large element of the children's own choice governing the matter. One recent author even prefers to speak of the 'untimetabled' day rather than the integrated day.[1] In consequence, there is a more or less wide variety of different activities to be found going on simultaneously in the room: some children may be reading or writing, others weighing or measuring, some painting, experimenting or modelling, while yet others may be in a group being instructed or questioned by the teacher, or out of the room altogether.

This then is what we might call the *minimum concept* of the integrated day. In practice, however, even with the most integrated of days there is almost inevitably some degree of formal timetabling. This is where the use of common and shared resources is involved, as with physical education, music and the use of television. The minimum concept of the integrated day, then, is that of a school day so organized that there are no, or at least very few, uniform and formalized breaks in the activities of learning and teaching, but rather a variety of such activities going on simultaneously and changing very much at the choice of the individual child, or perhaps of the group.

That the integrated day is indeed an organizational concept of this kind is confirmed both by observation and by the relevant though somewhat scanty literature on the subject. For instance, Brown and Precious say that 'the integrated day could be described as a school day which is combined into a whole and has the minimum of timetabling.'[2] These authors further explain that they have in mind what they call a 'natural flow of interest and activity'. Much the same view is held by a recent writer in *Forum*:

> The major contribution of the pattern of the integrated day, it
> would seem, is that it facilitates a simultaneous diversity of activities
> within a classroom and thus at any given time a wider range of
> choice for the children than is otherwise available.[3]

Interestingly, the Plowden Report neither indexes nor apparently mentions the term 'integrated day'. The nearest approach to it is in paragraph 536, where the committee discusses an integrated curriculum and the 'free day'. It seems doubtful that this omission from the report is due to any fastidiousness over the use of vague but fashionable terms. If anything, it probably testifies to the recency with which the term 'integrated day' has emerged into the dim light but great noise of educational fashion. In the slightly later Gittins Report (the Welsh version of Plowden), the integrated day does make one very brief appearance.

A point stressed earlier in constructing a conceptual map of a school was that organizational concepts are closely interrelated with those of aim, curriculum and method. This is true also of the concept of the integrated day. But the ideas on aims, methods and curriculum which are compatible with the minimum concept of the integrated day are very various. It is this classification under a single label of both similar and dissimilar practices which makes the notion so vague and confusing. For instance, in the book mentioned earlier, Brown and Precious do not describe just what is *specific* to the integrated day, but elaborate on more or less everything which either does or ideally would go on in their school. This means that a great many of the things that they describe could be and often are to be found even in quite traditional classrooms. We need to think, I suggest, on the one hand of what I have called a minimum concept, and on the other hand of very various and rather different ways in which this minimum can be enriched. As with cars, there is the basic model plus a wide variety of optional extras. The integrated curriculum and team teaching are two such extras, I maintain, which are often confusedly thought to be an essential part of an integrated day.

An integrated curriculum

Does the integrated day require an integrated curriculum? The clear answer to this question would seem to be negative. A classification of observed practice into four broad types of integrated day soon confirms this. School A thinks of the curriculum as very definitely divided up into more or less traditional subject areas, but a general feature of its methods of teaching is to set individual and group assignments rather than to engage in teaching the whole class. The children freely choose when and in what order they will complete their assignments, what they will do when their assignments are completed for the day, and when they will break off for some play. Here there is an integrated day with predominantly a subject curriculum. School B, on the other hand, sets no assignments and there is freedom of choice according to interest, but the classroom and its resources are arranged in bays or corners devoted to such subjects as mathematics, science, English, and art and craft, with a further corner for the classroom library. The children's activities are therefore still channelled, though indirectly, in the direction of a differentiated curriculum.

School C has no assignments, there is freedom of choice according to interest, and a changing variety of resources in each room is arranged and rearranged to suit actual or imputed interests as these wax and wane. Here is one sort of integrated curriculum and a regime that might most properly be labelled the 'free day'. It rests very much on views about the educative functions of play and is much more likely to be found in infant than in junior schools. Finally, School D has an integrated *half* day, and it will hardly need saying which half will in that case be integrated. In the morning, differentiated activities are engaged in related to development of the basic skills.

An integrated curriculum would therefore clearly seem to be an optional extra so far as the integrated day is concerned. And at this point I would like briefly to support an unfavourable judgment on a *wholly* integrated curriculum, whatever mixtures may have more to be said for them. But before supporting such a judgment, there is a general comment that deserves to be made. A characteristic feature of discussions of the integrated day, as of many discussions on important alternatives in educational practice, is a simplification of the issues into just two alternatives. Either we do the good thing, glowing with every virtue, exhibiting sound common sense and having an imagined majority on our side, or we must contemplate the worst depths of ignorance and wickedness. And so in the present debate we are likely to be invited to compare the very best of the integrated day with the very worst of unenlightened, backwater formal teaching, or a similarly unfair comparison will be made with vice and virtue the other way round. Looking at it this way saves all the trouble of being fair and gives powerful emotional reinforcement for carrying on with what we are doing already. The style is everywhere evident, and perhaps it has some place, but it ought not to be called argument. For my own part, both the very best and the very worst schools that I have seen recently have had some form of integrated day.

But returning to the question of how we are to estimate an integrated curriculum, as one of the optional extras, the following needs to be said. I have tried to show elsewhere,[4] with acknowledgment to Professor P. H. Hirst, that not every possible division of the curriculum into learning areas is arbitrary, or merely conventional, or just traditional. Admittedly many divisions into subjects simply are inherited traditions, to be judged only by their usefulness or convenience. But it is also possible to think of the curriculum as aimed at developing, to whatever degree a child's abilities allow, a variety of different and distinct forms of understanding. These forms of understanding can be distinguished one from another partly by their different conceptual schemes, but more importantly by the different sorts of criteria used to validate their claims.

These distinct forms of understanding supply different sorts of explanation or justification for what we think. They make possible different kinds of interest, appreciation and experience. They mark different ways of being critical and different ways in which we can be curious, imaginative or creative. They are an evolving inheritance of points of view of such general relevance to all that we do, and to how we see our situation, that one would have thought their development in children provided the large core of educational aims in a general education. And then there are the basic skills, especially of language, without which hardly anything else of value can go on in school.

It may not be possible to show conclusively that these aims could not be achieved by an integrated as much as by a differentiated curriculum, but a wholly integrated curriculum seems unlikely to achieve them. Where is there any assurance of the balance and progression which such aims require? An integrated curriculum will necessarily be dominated by some other unifying interest, such as the theme of the project, or the child's special hobby, or the teacher's own bias of mind. No doubt there is room and indeed value, especially motivational value, in having something of these sorts of integrated learning activity as *part* of the curriculum, perhaps even as a large part in the early stages. But in general it is true to say that aims are not achieved unless we consciously have them, even though what we ought to have aimed at may occasionally result merely fortuitously. The upshot of this argument, then, is at least to raise grave suspicions about abandoning all differentiation in the curriculum, often for no better reason than that some traditional subject divisions are seen to be arbitrary. Attention should at least first be drawn to the claims of a not merely conventional division of the curriculum into some five or six basic forms of understanding, plus the basic skills.

Team teaching

The second of the important optional extras earlier mentioned was team teaching. Does the integrated day require team teaching and the open plan architectural modifications which make team teaching possible? Of course, in one sense team teaching is required of the staff of any school. They have to cooperate with one another, accept some degree of direction from the headteacher and often also find ways of making any special teaching skills available to more children than they meet in their own particular classes. But something different from this is now meant by team teaching, and it is not the occasional secondary school practice of sharing the teaching of a large body of children with a group of teachers who give mass lessons followed up by class and small group activities.

By contrast with this, team teaching at the primary stage has come to mean sharing the teaching of larger groups of children than the traditional class. Learning then takes place in an open or openly interconnected space where the teachers move from individual to individual, or draw aside groups according to an overall and agreed programme. Something like the traditional class and its teacher may residually exist at the beginning and end of the day. This is the 'home base' from which children and teachers alike move out to wider contacts.

As soon as this organizational pattern is described, it can be seen to involve a version of the integrated day. But that does not mean that conversely the integrated day must always involve team teaching. In fact whereas the integrated day in one form or another seems to be increasingly widespread, team teaching is still a rarity, if only because of the obstacle to it which is presented in most schools by bricks and mortar. Not only can the integrated day exist apart from team teaching, but it can even exist in a single classroom while all the rest of the school is fairly traditional. So whereas we can say that where there is team teaching there will also be an integrated day, the converse is by no means true. Team teaching is an optional extra.

Is it desirable, even where bricks and mortar permit, that team teaching should accompany the integrated day? Again of course this is a matter of judgment, and indeed of balancing advantage and disadvantage rather than of identifying good and evil in any simple way. On the positive side, it may be said that team teaching greatly facilitates the easing of new and perhaps inexperienced teachers into the school, in that they can take on a full teaching load gradually, instead of all at once. The teachers can learn from seeing and hearing their colleagues, which is in fact often unavoidable in this situation. Again, taking small groups of children out of school on visits while the rest of one's class is left behind is greatly facilitated when there is joint supervision anyway.

The children, it may further be said, benefit in two main ways. As with family grouping, the older and younger can mix and help each other, though this may in practice appeal much more to the younger than to the older children. Also, the children have access to more teachers, with the possible benefits of some degree of semi-specialization.

But whatever the truth here, and experience alone can finally settle matters of fact, there seem equally disadvantages to team teaching. One wonders, for instance, whether being part of a mixed age group may not blur a child's age status and slow his progress to maturity. Just as in the family, parents may be oblivious to a child's growing up, and so treat him increasingly inappropriately, so too where all ages are mixed together teachers may be less attentive to children's changing needs as they grow up, and the children themselves may identify with those younger than themselves as equals. Moving up annually through classes, by contrast, emphasizes progressive maturity ('I'm in the third year now . . . we do . . . we have. . . .'). Some acute sociological observation rather than speculation is really needed on this point.

Again, if teachers' responsibilities are diffused across a large group rather than devoted for the most part to their own classes, may this not weaken each teacher's knowledge of, and commitment to, any particular children? As for the possessive pride which having one's own class may engender, even this has its positive side which perhaps more than offsets the irritations and jealousies which team teaching could produce. Another point is that team teaching requires much more co-operation between teachers. Not only does getting this cooperation raise difficulties of its own, but also it proliferates meetings and the keeping of written records, neither of which activities is itself teaching.

But perhaps the most ambiguous aspect of team teaching is the increased power which it gives the headteacher. Each teacher is made much more visible to him, and all but the detail of what is to be done may even be determined under his leadership at daily meetings. But individual teachers may have their own visions and ideals and acceptable eccentricities, and not wish to have their options restricted by being orchestrated into a uniform pattern of teaching. In those few team teaching schools personally known to me, I have been struck by the pattern of a strongminded and experienced headteacher, perhaps with an educational vision, who heads a team of young and receptive people plastic enough to take on his mould. This may be acceptable as an occasional pattern, but could hardly be a universal one without creating much friction through its infringement of the individual teacher's autonomy. Of course every headteacher has a right to expect some degree of cooperation and teamwork, but teachers as well as children differ in their natures.

A final point here is that increasing the power of the headteacher in this way lays the school wide open to his own almost inevitable biases, which in team teaching situations seem more often to be towards arts and crafts than towards mathematics and science. There may even be a reason for this, though again this is speculation, in the personality structure of those who opt for team teaching. But in conclusion, team teaching is indeed an option and is no more necessitated by an integrated day than is the option of having an integrated curriculum. Both are possible additions to what was earlier called the minimum concept.

Integration and streaming

What is there to be said for or against just the minimum concept of the integrated day, quite apart from the desirability or otherwise of such possible additions to it as an integrated curriculum or team teaching? Here of course, as with all such evaluation, there are two perennial difficulties. Plainly the question must turn in part on matters of fact: does or does not the practice achieve or realize the various desirable things that are expected of it? The difficulty here is not just that there is rarely any carefully controlled research on such large questions, but that even for those who observe or adopt the practice, there is a problem in the true perception of its results. To a varying degree we misperceive and misdescribe what is going on in our classrooms. Sometimes practitioners give rather woolly and lame accounts of what is in reality excellent practice, but sometimes also they are the victims of their own ideological self-deception in painting altogether too rosy a picture. And then there is the other difficulty of knowing which values or aims are to pick out these facts rather than those as the relevant ones, or these as the advantages and those as the dangers. With a little practice one quickly becomes sensitized to the value assumptions, often unconscious, made by witnesses, and perhaps also to some extent those made by oneself.

But to raise the practical question of what is to be said for or against the integrated day presupposes that we do indeed have a choice of what to do and only await sound arguments on the matter. If the issue is settled by factors outside our control, such as someone in authority, the physical arrangements or the unavailability of the relevant resources, then for us at least there is no practical question worth asking. Do we really have a choice where the integrated day is concerned? May it not be that such a choice is already preempted by decisions on the important question of streaming?

Streaming by ability as an organizational practice has of course recently come under heavy criticism, and in my own view rightly so. Streaming can be argued to rest on false psychological premises about the determinants and homogeneity of abilities in a child. It assumes abilities to be fixed early and highly correlated, so that children are classifiable into distinct kinds. Thus no second chance is given to those who have had an unfavourable home or school start, or who spent the minimum period in the infant school, and their early failures or disadvantages are soon institutionalized. Teachers greatly overestimate the extent to which transfer actually takes place between streams, and the stream label easily sets the teacher's expectations of the class and so tends to confirm the initial classification. Behaviour problems are created and concentrated in the low streams, and undesirable attitudes are produced in children and teachers alike throughout the school. Furthermore, since rather more than a small elite must now be educated, streaming does not even seem to be the best practice from the limited point of view of economic efficiency.

If the arguments against streaming are valid, then the usual alternative is to teach classes of mixed ability. This in turn sets severe limits to the effectiveness of class teaching. It requires instead more individualized curricula and methods of teaching, and an organization of learning and teaching which permits this. Although some functions for class teaching may still unashamedly remain and indeed have much merit, nevertheless for the most part, and especially in mathematics, learning must be thought of as an individual or small group activity. But while the teacher is dealing with one individual or group, he cannot be dealing with the others, so there must simultaneously be a mixture of activities only some of which are urgently teacher-demanding. Nor can the teacher be directing the other groups what to do all the time, so that more choice must be allowed if children are to be continuously occupied with something that they can involve themselves in.

But now we have more or less arrived, by a string of practical necessities consequent upon the decision not to stream, at the sort of arrangements earlier defined as the integrated day. A teacher is not perhaps unavoidably forced into this by not streaming, but it can be avoided only at a cost in terms of inefficiency of learning and loss of motivational involvement. Not streaming creates a very strong pressure towards having some form of integrated day. It is not surprising therefore that many schools have in fact arrived all unawares at some form of integrated day, and only *afterwards* learned that this is what it is called.

Some advantages and disadvantages

Yet whether there really is any choice in the matter of having an integrated day or not, clearly it will be introduced with more conviction if it has something positive to be said for it in its own right. There are at least three things that might be said in favour of it. First, more individualized learning in content and pace makes for more interest and involvement. When curricula and methods are more precisely tailored success is more likely, and it is hard to imagine anything at this stage more powerfully creative of favourable attitudes towards learning than success in it. But securing this advantage requires considerable organizational competence from the teacher, as well as suitable resources and straight teaching skill.

Second, since much learning must go on unsupervised while the teacher is restrictedly occupied with teacher-demanding activities, the children must in consequence be trained in learning how to learn for themselves in those parts of the curriculum where this is in fact possible. At the primary stage, this principally means acquiring various information-getting skills such as are involved in using reference books, using libraries and writing to relevant people. It involves also acquiring habits of initiative and persistence, so that available opportunities to find out for oneself are not shied away from, either out of timidity or out of the perception that it will involve going to some trouble.

These last remarks lead on to the third point that more

individualized learning, and developing the skills of learning for oneself, are closely connected with developing what I regard as a prime virtue to be aimed at: that of personal autonomy, or self-direction. Briefly, I would say that a person is autonomous in some understood context to the degree — and it is very much a matter of degree — that what he thinks and does is to be explained by reference to his own independent judgment: his deliberations, intentions, choices, decisions, attempts to understand, reflecting, planning and so on. Not only is there much satisfaction in a life which exhibits this virtue but, when it is moralized, it is at least part of the foundation of individual dignity. Responsibility then becomes individualized as a person becomes an agent in his own right, whose mind and actions are not explained just by reference to the pressures and influences of others. But autonomy is indeed a virtue, and although it has a natural basis in self-assertion, it yet needs its own kind of firm training, guidance and encouragement. Left to themselves many children will not naturally develop this virtue, but instead passively watch their friends, copy out word for word large lumps of text, and generally choose the easiest and most gratifying course that suggests itself. Every kind of organization in a school calls for its own appropriate training, in the children as much as in the teachers. Without this, what was indeed possible will not in fact be realized.

As well as possible advantages, there are also some possible dangers to be noticed in having an integrated day. How is balance and progression concerning the curriculum to be secured when the scope of individual choice is enlarged? In the fashion to throw out frameworks as rigid barriers, or as artificial or watertight compartments, it has gone unnoticed that frameworks can protect as well as restrict. They can save the individual from his own biases and from losing his direction in largely immediate practical preoccupations. In this connection, the tendency to favour the arts and crafts at the expense of mathematics and science has already been mentioned.

Another possible danger with the integrated day, as indeed with any innovations, is that, in McLuhan's phrase, 'the medium' may become 'the message'. And so, for example, French may be rejected from the curriculum not on the basis of its own merits or demerits, but on the grounds that it is against the spirit of the integrated day, or is out of line with the more individualized modes of learning presupposed by an integrated day. Again, teachers may be made to feel guilty about formal instruction even when this is appropriate, as with handwriting for example. A more adequate and generous view of aims is thus lost sight of in pursuit of doctrinal purity, and in an area which does not even directly represent an aim but rather just a pattern of organization.

But perhaps it is needless to expand further on what is only possible. Something positive, at least, has been said by way of contribution to the debate on the integrated day by suggesting how a minimum concept can be defined, and showing how this is related or unrelated to such other aspects of schools as an integrated curriculum, team teaching and streaming. Beyond that, it is hardly worth labouring the point that success or failure will depend on the energy, competence and insight with which individual teachers choose or are required to introduce this innovation. In practice the integrated day may represent anything from an embryonic university to a state of affairs someone recently described as being like 'a wet playtime all day'.

Chapter eight

Reading and research

Not every question that can sensibly be asked about reading is a question for psychology, though plainly many of the questions of greatest practical importance can properly be answered only by that science. But just as it is important that psychologists should try to answer some of the questions raised by difficulties and failures encountered by children in learning to read, so also is it important, if confusions are to be avoided, that their questions should be correctly identified, and that the place of their answers in coming to educational decisions should be properly located. Let me expand on each of these two requirements.

An obvious point on which we ought to be clear in thinking about reading is just what this activity called 'reading' *is*. What do we *mean* by 'reading'? How should we characterize it? Now in spite of the fact that many of them supply erudite answers to it, this is not in fact a psychologist's question, or rather not his any more than anybody else's. It is a question of meaning which calls for a conceptual clarification, not a question of fact calling for references to research. If such a question is not correctly identified, the answer offered may, perhaps, be some such behaviouristic revelation as that reading is really a sequence of vocal or sub-vocal responses to printed visual stimuli, or something of that sort. If I may quote Traxler: 'Specialists in the reading field think of "reading" as anything from a set of more or less mechanical habits to something akin to the "thinking" process itself.'[1] Questions of conceptual clarification, however, are questions of a sort with which philosophers very much occupy themselves these days, as indispensable preliminaries to their further inquiries. It would seem appropriate enough, therefore, if I should begin by suggesting a characterization of what is meant when we talk about 'reading'.

The second matter of importance that I said it would be well to be clear about was the proper location of research findings in the process of coming to practical decisions in education. It seems sometimes to be thought that psychologists can, by themselves, settle what decisions ought to be made, or can, by themselves, tell the teacher what he ought or ought not to do. But this is just not so, and the reason why it is not so is not just that a certain freedom for teachers is institutionally safeguarded; indeed, it would be an abuse of that freedom arbitrarily to reject such findings as have been established. Nor is it the fact that any important piece of educational research usually rests on assumptions, the questioning of which can always provide an escape route for anyone who dislikes the research findings.

The reason why psychologists can never by themselves settle what ought to be done derives partly from certain logical features of reasoning to a practical conclusion, and partly from the fact that sociologists, administrators and others also have voices to raise, and these voices ought to be heard. For example, a psychologist might show that many children can be taught to read quite some time before the start of formal schooling. But so what? Such findings can have no possible practical relevance unless they are addressed to people who, on quite separate grounds, consider it *desirable* to move in the direction shown to be possible. Some might consider that very young children should be occupied with other things than with reading, even if that is possible for them.

The proper location of psychological research findings in the process of arriving at practical decisions is by no means an obvious one, and to talk of the 'curricular implications' of research findings conceals all sorts of logical difficulties. If a research such as that into i.t.a. is considered *by itself,* it has no 'implications' whatever for what we ought or ought not to do. To have such implications its findings must be taken together with premises of a very different sort, premises which reflect the different interests different people might have in this research. Only when taken together with various other such premises can a piece of research be said to have 'implications'. The appraisal of the logic of various forms of reasoning, however, is again something with which philosophers concern themselves. It would further seem appropriate, therefore, if I took up this problem in the second half of my paper. But to turn first to the question of what we *mean* by reading, I must begin with some remarks on the concept of an 'activity'.

Reading

There are always at least two ways in which we can regard any human activity. First of all, we can regard it from the point of view of those engaged in it, as persons conscious of being in a particular situation, and conscious also of doing, or trying to do, various things. From this point of view, also, we can appraise what people do as correct or incorrect, intelligent or foolish, right or wrong, intentional or unintentional, and we can ask them their reasons for doing what they do.

The second way in which we can regard any human activity is in terms of its physical and physiological accompaniments: the bodily motions involved, sensory and neural activity, the activation of speech organs in vocalizing and so on. To regard human activity in this way is to view it through behaviouristic spectacles, which has many advantages for methodology but is pernicious if the spectacles become contact lenses.

Another way in which this distinction can be brought out is as follows. What is to do the 'same thing' on two occasions? This question cannot be answered unless it is first specified in what respect the two occasions are to be regarded as the same. And this specification will be different according to whether it is in respect of the conscious intention of the person that we are comparing the two occasions, or in respect of his bodily motion, vocalizings and so on. For example, think of a child going through Schonell's Graded Word Reading Test. Is he doing the same thing in saying the first words he pronounces correctly as in saying the last words he pronounces correctly, for example in correctly saying 'tree' and 'egg' as in correctly saying 'somnambulist' or 'ineradicable'? If we regard him just as a vocalizer, then no doubt he is doing the same thing, in that on both occasions he sounds what is there in a way which *we* regard as correct. But from *his* point of view, as a conscious person, he may be, and in fact usually is, doing two quite different things: in the first case, saying what he himself recognizes and knows to be a word, and in the second case something less: merely blending the sounds he knows are appropriate to certain shapes. A score on such a test therefore represents a curious mixture of things. In teaching there is always the possibility of this kind of discrepancy between what a child is actually doing and the interpretation we place on his behaviour.

The first step towards characterizing reading as an activity is to see that such a characterization must be from the point of view of the person who is reading, not from the point of view of the behaviourist. Reading is something which we do correctly or incorrectly, intelligently or stupidly, rightly or wrongly, and such adverbs can be applied only to conscious performances. To characterize reading, then, we need not waste time in considering vocalizings, eye-movements, twitchings of the larynx and other such phenomena as may accompany it. But even from the conscious person's point of view several possibilities remain open and to consider them in turn will usefully take us over disputed ground.

Plainly, reading is not just recognizing the sounds appropriate to the letters discriminated by us, nor even blending those sounds properly. Such an ability in phonic analysis may well be a necessary condition of efficient word-recognition, but is not by itself even that. In the former example, a child correctly saying 'somnambulist' or 'ineradicable' would only be taking it on trust that these actually were words, and not just nonsense put in front of him for some reason best known to adults. Word-recognition implies the *foreknowledge* of a word, which is now identified in print by means of such clues as can be mustered. So a child's correct sounding may or may not also be word-recognition, depending on how *he* sees what he is doing.

Then is word-recognition reading? There are times, it is true, when our eagerness to detect signs of progress leads us to call this 'reading', but to call word-recognition 'reading' is like calling the isolated naming activities of very young children 'talking': it is to be poised at the very edge of the area covered by a concept. This can easily be seen from the following cases. You could go through a book backwards, from bottom to top and right to left, recognizing all the words there perfectly correctly, but we should hardly call this 'reading', and certainly not 'reading the book'. Nor would it be any adequate reply to the question 'Have you read so-and-so?' to say that you recognized every word in it. There can be no doubt, however, that continuous word-recognition is a necessary *part* of the process of reading, because 'reading' shares with the verbs of perception the double feature of making some kind of

101

knowledge-claim on the one hand, and indicating at the same time the basis of the claim on the other. For example, to say that you can 'hear' something is first of all to claim to have identified a certain object, say a mosquito, and secondly to indicate that you identified it on the basis of certain sounds. Analogously, reading is making some kind of knowledge-claim on the basis of word-recognition.

What kind of knowledge-claim is implied by reading then? Evidently it is that the *meaning* of the text is being grasped. There is, therefore, a curious redundancy in talking of 'reading for meaning' as people often do. It is comparable to such pleonasms as 'dreaming dreams' and 'seeing sights', though perhaps it serves as a useful slogan, when people are too preoccupied with phonic analysis or word-recognition, to remind them of the nature of the activity they are so earnestly about. Adding this to the earlier result then, we can now say that reading is a conscious activity in which we grasp the meaning of a text through a process of continuous word-recognition. With increasing skill, of course, consciousness is focused more and more on grasping meaning, until word-recognition is not itself consciously attended to at all, which is why so-called proof-reading is so difficult an art.

Meaning

But now more must be said about this unanalysed phrase 'grasping meaning'. What *is* this meaning that we grasp? The necessarily incomplete answer is that it is an *appropriate* meaning which we grasp in this way. The incompleteness of such a word as 'appropriate' here is unavoidable because what *is* appropriate varies enormously with what the text is *about*, how language is being intentionally used in it and the level and sort of comprehension being demanded, but in spite of this diversity there is something further that can fairly briefly be said.

The 'meaning' which is to be grasped in reading is there to be grasped because there was a meaningful use of language by someone which is here symbolically recorded. That use of language by someone consisted of the deployment of concepts to some purpose: to describe, request, warn, insult, order and so on. So that for anyone to succeed in reading a particular text it is necessary that he should understand the concepts being deployed and the purpose behind their use. Whether he will succeed in doing that is not just a question of alphabets, words in colours, big print or any other aids to word-recognition: it is a question of his general mental development. I should like to make two comments by way of expanding on this a little.

First, since reading essentially involves grasping the way in which language is being meaningfully used, we cannot be said to be 'reading' *before* we understand how language is meaningfully used. We cannot be said to be reading, for example, when someone of a behaviouristic frame of mind teaches us, at the age of fourteen months, to discriminate and respond to funny shapes – shapes which adults, did we but know it, call letters and words. Just conceivably such a training in discrimination and response might prove to have been of value when *later* our mental development makes 'reading' a possibility, but it is not itself reading, and it can only cause confusion to pass it off as being so. Similarly, when later a child *has* begun to read, if we present him with material beyond his mental grasp, we may get him to do something which *looks* like reading, and which impresses those whose only wish is to be impressed, but that, too, cannot properly be called 'reading'. A necessary condition of being able to read anything is that our mental development be equal to grasping its meaning.

The second point is that once a child is reading material that requires only childhood commonsense to grasp, he is ready to use reading as itself a way of learning. Having learned to read, he is now ready to read to learn, and this will involve him in distinctive forms of critical thought, the specialized uses of language we call science, history, and so on.

I know that some people regard knowledge as an undifferentiated mush in which the only possible principle of division is into what interests you and what does not, and it would take a long time to show convincingly that, on the contrary, there are logically distinct forms of thought in the recognition of which there is nothing at all arbitrary or merely conventional. But on this occasion I shall have to take all that as established. In any case, Professor Hirst has set out the arguments for taking this view in a recent book.[2] Suffice it to say that forms of thought are not quite the same thing as subjects, since often several subjects exemplify only a single form, scientific thought for example. And further, I am not implying anything about being 'formal' or 'informal', 'watertight compartments', or any other such well-thumbed cards in the educational pack.

At this stage, the stage of reading to learn when the mechanics have been mastered, it is better to talk of study skills rather than of reading skills, for reasons that will become clear in a moment. It is the *effectiveness* of reading that matters now. But what is 'effective' reading? Something fairly platitudinous might be said, such as that effective reading involves adjusting speed and closeness of attention to one's purpose in reading and the difficulty of the text. But effective reading is also very *different* things in *different* forms of thought, and if this kind of reading is regarded as something for reading specialists to make overall pronouncements upon, either platitude or distortion will surely be the result. We shall be told that effective reading is first having a rapid preview, next posing questions, then reading the text and finally summarizing it, or something of that sort. No doubt such a prescription fits some things well enough, but not others, not poetry for example.

If I may enter a general caution at this point, talk about 'effective reading' shares a lack of clarity also to be found in talk about 'effective thinking', 'creativity', 'showing imagination' and 'using intelligence'. Such expressions easily conceal from us that the criteria for their application are very different in different fields of thought and action. We may slide into thinking that here are unitary goals for us to aim at in educating children, that because you can be imaginative both in science and in poetry they must be much more similar than it would seem, for example. This is a mistake, and one which vitiates even high-level reports. With words of appraisal such as 'effective', 'imaginative', 'creative' and 'intelligent', one has to distinguish their formal meaning from their variable criteria of application, and it is the very variable criteria of application which do all the hard work. Not seeing this is, I think, behind much of the muddle about intelligence and the conflicting definitions of it that are offered.

But to return to the question of reading, it would not be adequate to admit that there are, of course, *two* sorts of reading, reading for enjoyment and reading for information, and then to confine one's remarks to the latter. For first of all, there is no reason to suppose that nobody enjoys being informed; and secondly, it scarcely does justice to fiction to regard it as being able to do nothing for us beyond giving pleasure, or justice to non-fiction to regard it as just a lot of information, moreover, information no part of which has an educational priority over any other part.

No doubt this distinction to which I am drawing attention, between the different *sorts* of study skills appropriate to different *forms* of thought, is much more important at the secondary stage, but administrative breaks ought not to be thought of as educational chasms, and what is writ large at the secondary stage ought already to be beginning to be differentiated out at the primary junior stage. For example, to study the properties of magnets is in many important ways different from studying the history of number and that from studying cocoa-farming in Ghana. Reading Walter de la Mare's poem 'The Listeners' is different again, and this in turn is not quite the same as reading a story, say by Paul Berna.

But to return to the characterization of reading as grasping the *appropriate* meaning of a text, enough has now been said to justify the incompleteness of that description. Appropriateness can vary not only with the purpose for which language is being used in the text, but also with the sorts of concept being deployed and the form of thought to which they belong. Reading to learn is not munching away at an undifferentiated mush, but an advance into quite distinct sorts of understanding, each requiring a different frame of mind and different kinds of appraisal. Once children are able to read, the educational task is gradually to introduce them to these different forms of understanding. Insensitivity to these differences can have quite grotesque results, such as in treating W. H. Auden's poem 'Night Mail' as a piece of information about the workings of the Post Office.

Educational decisions

I want now to take up the second of the two main questions I posed at the beginning. The question was: 'What is the logical relation between such findings as research may establish and practical judgments about what we ought to do?' Or alternatively: 'What is the proper location of research findings in drawing practical conclusions in education?' What I want to try to shed some light on is the logic of drawing such a conclusion, first in general terms and then more particularly in drawing conclusions about reading.

It can be seen at once, I think, that two quite different *sorts* of premises are required for this: first, value-judgments as to what it would be worth doing, or what is educationally desirable, and secondly, technical commentaries of various kinds on such judgments. Practical conclusions are to be derived from a weighing of these two different sorts of premises. Let me expand on each kind a little.

By a 'value-judgment', I mean here a judgment to the effect that something or other would be well *worth* doing, or that from an educational point of view it would be highly *desirable,* or more simply that it would be a *good* thing to do. Of course, it is possible to make negative value-judgments as well as positive ones, or indeed judgments of indifference, but I shall not go into any of those complications.

Positive value-judgments are inescapable in coming to educational decisions. The concept of education itself implies them, as Professor Peters has made clear, since the worthwhileness, the value, of doing something is one of the criteria which have to be satisfied if a process is to be counted as 'educational' at all.[3] Value-judgments relate as much to the procedures permissible in schools as to the kinds of learning that those procedures are designed to achieve. A final point to notice about value-judgments is that it is our wanting to do such things as these judgments prescribe which gives practical force to the conclusions we draw. Without them, we should have no reason for acting, and all the technical commentaries of psychologists, sociologists and others would be so much chatter, of theoretical interest perhaps, but of no practical relevance. Value-judgments provide the criterion of relevance for technical commentaries, and the practical force of the conclusions drawn.

So much for the first sort of premise we require if we are to draw practical conclusions: the second sort I shall characterize only briefly. The second class of premises we require consists of such technical commentaries as have already been mentioned, the commentaries of psychologists, sociologists and administrators, for example. These describe what would be an efficient way of doing what we want to do, how failures are to be avoided, the feasibility of the organization required, the possible consequences of proposals, and so on. On all such questions of fact, the commentary of experts is relevant and appropriate. But such commentary has neither relevance nor any kind of 'implication' for educational practice unless it is addressed to the pursuit of an activity judged to be worthwhile on educational grounds. With research into problems that have been *set* by education, such as some of the research into reading, spelling, mathematics teaching or moral education, there is no problem, since comment derives its point from, and is addressed to, some aspect of a worthwhile educational activity right from the start. But with research which derives its point from some problem *within* a particular discipline, such as much of learning theory for example, it may be hard indeed to find any kind of relevance to education in it. Human activities might then be isolated from their context in a distinctive form of social life, with all the troublesome contaminating effects which that has, and *redescribed* in such a way as to present them as being in no important way different from the behaviour of rats, cats, pigeons and monkeys. The relevance of such researches to education would then be quite easy to show, except that 'education' would itself have become something different in the process of redescription.

It would be false to suppose, however, that premises of *either* of these two kinds can have practical implications without consideration of the others. For example, what is judged to be worthwhile may evoke an administrative commentary which, in the light of other value-judgments, rules it out as impractical, for instance, pulling down buildings to suit some desirable reorganization. Again, a technical commentary by a psychologist may be dismissed as putting forward a procedure of teaching which conflicts with what is judged to be a desirable manner in which to educate people, or as requiring equipment that is too expensive.

When a tentative practical conclusion *is* reached, however, it has to be further examined by a technical commentary on its probable consequences if adopted, and by a fresh evaluation of those consequences. One can see, then, that though it may be possible to set out in logical order the reasons which justify a conclusion *after* it has been reached, rules for *reaching* such conclusions could scarcely be more than cautionary. This inescapability of making complex practical judgments in education is analogous to the position which the politician finds himself in. He too has certain desirable aims in mind, things which it would be valuable to do; but he too must listen to the commentaries of experts, such as economists, lawyers and administrators, and in the end he too has to arrive, in a limited time and usually on limited evidence, at a practical judgment for which no precise guiding rules can be given.

No doubt if teachers and headteachers, or indeed politicians, had to start from scratch, arrive at many different kinds of value-judgments and appraise a mass of relevant technical commentary on them before drawing any practical conclusions, they would achieve little in a lifetime. But in reality, of course, such practical judgments as have to be made are always made against a background of what may be called 'existing practice', in which ways of doing things have already been worked out and institutionalized as curricula, buildings, procedures, and so on. This is why new ideas, whether on reading or anything else, never achieve anything overnight: they can never at first match the detailed working out and guidance of existing practice. And if this is a nuisance to people with good new ideas, it is also a blessing when ideas of other sorts appear, and it serves to carry the enterprise forward still if we are uncertain which are which.

With these general remarks as a guide on the two kinds of premises required to make practical judgments, I should like now to return to the particular case of decisions about reading. The first thing to be considered will be judgments about the educational *value* of reading, and there are, I think, three main arguments that can be given to show the value of reading, each of them deriving from a consideration of what it is to be educated, not from a consideration of the dubious merits of later being able to read income tax forms and the like.

Decisions about reading

The first argument rests on the importance of reading as a way of learning. In an earlier section of this paper I described reading to learn as an advance into quite distinct sorts of understanding, each requiring a different frame of mind and different kinds of appraisal. Such an advance is a very large part of what we mean when we speak of children's intellectual development. No doubt some progress could be made without books, as it often had to be in medieval times before printing, but books free the child of dependence on the time, patience and availability of others, and enable him to go ahead on his own and when he likes, in school and out of it. However, books do more than conveniently *supplement* what the teacher says. They have a very important function to fulfil in providing knowledge which may *conflict* with what the teacher or others say, so that a step, even if only a small one, is taken away from reliance on authorities towards a more critical acceptance of what is offered. Even infants can detect inconsistency.

Second, reading is valuable not only as a fresh access to knowledge and as an extension of experience, but also as a medium of instruction. No doubt speech is the critical language skill here, as any teacher of immigrant children soon vividly realizes, but if teaching and learning are to be individualized, or done by groups, as many would advocate that they should be in the primary school, then the ability to read instructions on the blackboard, in textbooks and on work-cards is indispensable. A teacher must be able to leave one group in order to attend to others.

Third, a child who cannot read is necessarily a child who cannot write, so that all forms of written work are barred from him too, especially work based on topics which require the use of the classroom library. Yet writing is an important way of making thought definite and of articulating coherently our personal experience. Both for personal writing and for more impersonal work, therefore, writing is crucially important in school.

On the question of *value,* then, there is no difficulty in showing the desirability of learning to read and of reading to learn. Of all the judgments of educational value that have to be made, this is one of the easiest. Reading is so important, in fact, that one would have thought it an unquestionable presumption that children would make as early a start as possible in school, though admittedly that is *only* a presumption and might have to be qualified, at least in the case of some children, by technical commentary on it.

There is, however, a view which lays much less value than this on reading, a view which regards it as somehow 'unnatural' for children, especially in the infant school, to be much concerned with books; rather they should be *growing*—something that one would have thought was in any case inevitable. Historically, the basis of this objection is not in the first instance to be found in any findings of research, though these may be brought in to defend it, so much as in an imagined bond of sympathy with the child, who is seen, or rather felt, to be struggling to realize his inner nature in the face of the artificialities imposed on him by insensitive teachers too preoccupied with learning. This conception of the child goes back to Froebel and earlier still to Rousseau. For example, in Rousseau's *Emile,* after learning that 'reading is the curse of childhood', we come to the following passage:

The hour strikes, the scene is changed. All of a sudden his eye grows dim, his mirth has fled. Farewell mirth, farewell untrammelled sports in which he delighted. A stern, angry man takes him by the hand, saying gravely, 'Come with me, sir', and he is led away. As they are entering the room, I catch a glimpse of books. Books, what dull food for a child of his age! The poor child allows himself to be dragged away; he casts a sorrowful look on all about him, and departs in silence, his eyes swollen with the tears he dare not shed, and his heart bursting with the sighs he dare not utter.[4]

No doubt if we penetrated the fog of sentimentality surrounding this statement, we also would deplore the sort of teaching, and the kind of books used for it, by which Rousseau was so revolted. But the obvious answer is to improve the manner of teaching and to design books more suitable for young children, both of which things have now been done, instead of having poor Emile arrive at twelve years of age scarcely knowing what a book is, or having his modern counterpart otherwise occupied till he shows signs of *wanting* to read.

The idea of reading as somehow opposed to the young child's 'nature', or not being in the main stream of 'growth', dies hard. Yet a break with anything that could coherently be called 'nature' was already being made at the age of two, when the child was emerging from a biologically orientated condition into a form of social life, through the learning of language. As Professor Hampshire puts it:

At any time after infancy we are looking at a world already divided for us into persisting things of many different types, and with our attention already fixed upon a particular range of resemblances. In any man's experience, Nature has always been overlaid by, and approached through, a set of social conventions, the conventions of a language in being.[5]

If reading is to be condemned as 'unnatural', therefore, so also must speech be, because in that too we are 'unnatural', and writing must share the same fate. In fact, if the implications of concepts such as 'nature' were consistently thought out, we should, I think, have to return to the forests of the not-so-noble savages.

Nor is a concept such as that of 'growth' in any better case. The slightest acquaintance with anthropology is enough to show that children are quite unlike acorns, which need only a favourable environment in order to develop into splendid oaks. The way in which children develop is very much a function of the social expectations that surround them. Arriving at the stage of wanting to read is not the budding of a latent interest, analogous to the appearance of a new twig on a growing oak, but is very much a matter of what adults are perceived to value. And I have given arguments for thinking that reading is one thing that they ought very much to value.

The doctrine of 'growth' would seem to offer no good reason for denying the great *value* of an early start in reading, as a very strong presumption to be weighed against such technical commentary as is clear on this. However, such value-judgments as have so far been made do not by themselves settle what we ought to do, and speaking generally now, if we are to come to any working conclusions about reading, at *least* the following four kinds of commentary are necessary: first, commentaries on any psychological and physiological conditions which may clearly be shown to be necessary for making a good start, on the relative merits of different methods of teaching and on the differences in effectiveness of using different kinds of media, such as i.t.a., *Words in Colour,* film and so on; secondly, sociological commentaries on class differences in parents' and pupils' expectations concerning the role of the school in learning to read, and the place of reading in education; thirdly, administrative commentaries on book and equipment allowances and staffing; and finally, there will always be purely local considerations such as the amount of experience of a particular staff, size of classes, materials available, language background of new entrants and so on. With the various issues separated out in this way there are, I think, several points on which one can be much clearer.

First, when there are so many considerations to be taken into account it is scarcely surprising that different people come to quite different practical conclusions, and without any inconsistency between them. Not only do premises enter into the reasoning of teachers in some areas which quite properly would have no place in the reasoning of others, but also the weight attached to different premises varies considerably. It is hardly to be supposed, therefore, that any particular piece of research will provide knock-down arguments for everyone to take a particular course, unless a very dubious 'other things being equal' clause is added.

Second, and this I think is most important, even a large-scale experiment such as that with the Initial Teaching Alphabet will have results which, taken *by themselves,* can have no direct implications whatever for the curriculum. It can furnish a technical commentary to be taken into account in developing a practical programme, but the educational values supplying the practical force behind developing such a programme will be arrived at in quite another way than by experiment. If the matter seems otherwise, it is likely that a good many assumptions are unconsciously being made, and two sorts of muddle will be apt to result. On the one hand it may be thought that experiment settles everything and that for anyone doubtful about the *value* of doing something the proper course is to 'see what research shows'. On the other hand, research itself can only suffer if it is clouded by quite separate issues.

Third, and following on from that, a research such as that into i.t.a. can therefore have a quite different interest for people interested in developing different sorts of programme. For example, people who regard reading as so important as to think that the climate of expectation in schools should be one in which it would be a surprising fact about a child if he had not yet begun learning to read, though a fact which in some cases could no doubt be justifiably explained — such people will see i.t.a. as pointing to the making of a brisk start with five-year-olds. Others, whose main interest is in the earlier opportunity to do some worthwhile writing, both personal writing and writing of a more impersonal sort on factual topics, will see in that the relevance of the speeded progress made with i.t.a. But the main interest of these experiments derives not so much from the value of a brisk start, or from the worthwhileness of the writing made possible, but from the value of reading itself in education. What that value is I have already tried to make clear in terms of the kinds of understanding which enter into intellectual development.

Chapter nine

Competition in education

Competition is a topic which has been all but totally ignored in the educational literature of recent years. And this neglect is surprising, since competition is evident in our educational arrangements at many points. There is competition for class positions and grammar school places, for prizes and entrance to universities, to be first, best, top, fastest and so on. Opinions divide, and hackles quickly rise, over the virtues and vices of such arrangements as these, but the attitudes expressed typically cluster with attitudes to other things in a way which has conveniently been called child-centred or traditional. At one extreme, competition is regarded with horror and much is said about the virtues of cooperation. At the other extreme one finds the tough-minded Black Paper approval of competition as a crucial necessity, not just in schooling but in life generally.

Clearly there will be points in this controversy at which factual findings should be decisive. An instance would be whether some form of competition does or does not in fact have certain envisaged consequences. Yet one suspects in advance that here is a topic which could be seen as giving some persuasive force to an emotive theory of ethics. Facts there may be, but in the end divergences of attitude may well remain which can rationally be neither justified nor attacked: they just are the attitudes of those who express them. But before that stage of irreconcilable difference is reached, if it must be reached, there is much scope for rational argument and not only argument over the truth or falsity of research findings. There are, for instance, at least two conceptual questions which can be rationally pursued, and with some profit, before the value question is faced. These two conceptual questions concern what competition is, and what things can in consequence be competed for.

What is competition?

I take as a conveniently simple schema for analysis and discussion the situation where A and B are in competition for X. In this schema, A and B will normally be individuals, or else associations of individuals such as schools, classes, houses, teams, companies, or nations. Nevertheless, theories, policies and ideals may also properly be said to be in competition with each other when they are canvassed or championed by people as being singularly entitled to be called true, correct, right or perhaps most suitable for funding. But granted this conveniently simplifying schema, I want to suggest three conditions as being separately necessary and jointly sufficient for A and B to be in competition for X.

First of all, A and B must both want X. There must be some common object desired by both, such as the best seat, Mary's favours, the largest share in the market, the job just advertised, the prize, to be first away from the traffic lights, to sit nearest to God, and so on. For without a common object the paths of A and B will not necessarily cross.

The second condition is that A's gaining possession of X must exclude B's gaining possession of it. For if both A and B can have their desires satisfied, e.g. because Mary has an identical twin sister or because there is a whole row of the best seats still vacant, then there is no need for or point in competition. Thus we do not normally compete for air to breathe since there is enough available for everyone. But in a wrecked submarine or a collapsed coalmine there could conceivably be competition, and the space in which to enjoy fresh air, or in which to enjoy the air on the upwind side of a big city, are often very much competed for.

Yet a third condition is that both A and B should persist in trying to gain exclusive possession of X even when they know that one of them must be excluded. They must become and remain competitors. For, realizing that they are in a situation of potential competition, A and B might both volunteer to forgo X, or agree to distribute it equally between them, or take turns in having it, instead of becoming competitors for its exclusive possession. These alternatives are common enough amongst friends, close colleagues and families. Of course, A and B may be in competition with each other without yet knowing it, as when institutions recruit from the same pool of ability without being aware of each other's existence. Companies seeking a particular market may have to do some market research to find out just who their competitors are, while Mary's several boy-friends may not even guess at first that they are in competition with anyone at all. This third condition, however, indicates what is necessary when A and B do know, or do find out.[1]

For A and B actually to be in competition for X, then, A and B must both want X, A's getting it must exclude B from having it, and they must both persist in trying to get it even if they know that one's getting it must exclude the other. When fifty pupils enter the school chess club's tournament, or when 1,000 eleven-year-olds sit the eleven-plus examination to determine the 250 of them who will go to grammar schools, we do indeed have a complication of the simple schema I have adopted for analysis, but nothing essential is changed. But before passing on to the second of the two conceptual questions raised at the beginning, there are some educationally relevant comments which can already be made in the terms of this suggested analysis.

It seems often to be assumed that competition and cooperation are themselves in competition with each other. To embrace the one, it is assumed, is wholly to exclude the other from a place in our educational arrangements. But this is manifestly not so. Competition does in fact normally require various forms of cooperation. Wherever A and B are groups of individuals, such as school houses or teams, then competitive advantages will usually accrue to the group which can muster a high degree of internal cooperation. The best football teams are not necessarily those composed of eleven star players. Furthermore, whether A and B are individuals or teams, they must normally cooperate with each other at least in observing the rules governing the competition. These rules may be the conventional rules of a game, the rules of war, State laws governing industrial and commercial practices, or school rules related to some test situation. Even when competitive testing in a classroom reaches such a pitch that each child jealously guards what he writes with a hedge of books and crooked arms, still there are no-cheating rules to be jointly observed if the competition is to be fair. Competition, whatever one may think of it, does require cooperative observance of its own shared ethic in all cases short of total ruthlessness. Of course, it does make sense to urge the replacement of competition by a much greater degree of cooperation, but cooperation in less degree is still normally required where competition still prevails.

Those who wish to eliminate or greatly to reduce the amount of competition in education often make what they think is an important concession. Competition is all right, they say, provided that each child is competing only with himself. But is this a conceptual possibility if the earlier analysis is correct? Can one compete with oneself? Taken literally, competition with oneself would involve a contradiction: I myself must both win and lose in the same competition. If this contradiction is avoided by dissociating my present from my past self, then presumably it is not myself after all but someone else with whom I then compete. The reality of what is approved here, of course, is simply that I should now try to improve on my own past performances: I should try to play the piano better than I did last week, or try to get more sums right or to write more neatly. Doing one's best and trying to improve are doubtless central to learning situations, but they are not perspicuously described as competing with oneself.

Nevertheless, a reason can I think readily be discerned for favouring this illogical description. Consider an educational climate in which true competition is rife. If a reformer then wishes to shift the motivational emphasis away from interpersonal rivalry to a spirit of individual self-improvement, then the notion of 'competing with oneself' is an admirably persuasive device. Instead of blocking or opposing an existing attitude it seeks more economically to redirect it. Though strictly lacking in sense, the phrase may therefore be thought to be justified by its effects in helping to shift a well-entrenched practice towards something else thought to be more acceptable.

Close in spirit to competition, but not quite the same as it, is emulation. The emulous person strongly wishes to approach, or match, or even perhaps excel another person in some respect, for instance in abilities, achievements, position, or wealth. He takes another as a standard to try to equal or surpass. But this desire does not necessarily place the emulous and the emulated people in competition with each other. To try to emulate Russell's clarity, or Rothschild's business success, is not to try to gain exclusive possession of anything. But emulation is like competition in that what one thinks of it will probably be in part determined by one's opinion of the emotions by which it is normally accompanied, such as admiration or envy, liking or hatred.

What things can be competed for?

If the analysis of competition so far given is correct, then the range of possible objects of competition will be co-extensive with the range of things that can satisfy the three conditions laid down. Of these conditions, the first two seem by far the most important. That is to say, to be a possible object of competition something must (i) be capable of being desired, i.e. of being thought good, an advantage worth having, etc; and (ii) be capable of being exclusively possessed, whether by its very nature or by virtue of some rule or convention. For instance, in relation to being desired, it is hard to imagine how simple possession of a saucer of mud could be a possible object of competition, while the exclusiveness condition would find a difficulty in the idea of competing to believe that God exists. But the interesting question now is: can education be a possible object of competition?

Let us grant that being an educated person is certainly a state that can be desired. But can it be exclusively possessed? Roughly speaking, to be educated is to possess certain attitudes, knowledge and abilities, for instance to care about truth, to understand the principles of magnetism, or to be able to see irrelevance. These items are suggested as an indication of the general sort of thing, rather than as obviously essential items. But possessions of this mental sort do have two features which seem to rule them out as possible objects of competition. First, they are logically non-transferable. Though I may share with you my understanding of the Industrial Revolution, I cannot give it to you or be dispossessed of it as if it were a car, coat or can of beer. A second and closely related feature is that these mental possessions represent infinitely repeatable achievements. My possession of them in no way debars you from exactly similar achievements, within the limits of your personal educability. We can all know the facts about Tudor England, know the declension of *mensa*, believe in God, have the skill to play the violin, or respond appreciatively to literature, without exhausting a limited stock of anything. There are not fewer facts left for you to learn if I gorge myself on Tudor history, or less skill available for you if I quickly master the fingering of the 'cello.

These features of educational achievements should not be confused with the open-endedness of those same achievements. It may indeed be silly to think of anyone as having an absolutely complete knowledge of

117

history or science, since there will always be more that could be known. But it would not matter if there were only 148 historical facts that could be learned. The essential point is that this learning is infinitely repeatable, and not that what is learned is infinitely extendable.

A very similar point to that made here was also made by Spinoza in his *Ethics*. Spinoza argued there that virtue and happiness together lay in increasing our understanding of God-or-nature. But in that case, he further argued, 'the greatest good of those who follow virtue is common to all, and all can equally enjoy it'.[2] The greatest good in life was thus presented as a goal which could be pursued by all without competition or strife.

Being educated, then, is a state for which it makes no sense to compete, since it represents a logically nontransferable and an infinitely repeatable achievement. And this result, if it is true, seems to me interesting and important if we are to place competition in proper perspective in our educational arrangements. Nevertheless, since competition plainly does occur, it must obviously be capable of having some place in education. What place, then, could it have, if the state of being educated is not something for which it makes sense to compete?

There are, I think, two main ways in which competition can have a place in education. Each is related to one or other of the main conditions for being a possible object of competition, namely that an object be capable of being desired and that it be capable of being exclusively possessed. It would not be sensational news to any practising teacher to say that children do not always want to be educated, either at all or in some particular respect. If we nevertheless persist in the desire to educate them, there then faces us a serious motivational problem. And so arises one main way in which competition may enter education. We can so arrange things that educational achievements are inseparably linked with some other artificial achievements for which children can readily be induced to compete. We can thus hold out prizes, team points, privileges, places of prestige, carefully hoarded approval, or the bliss of being top or first or fastest as restricted rewards, available to some few who satisfy sufficiently, by their personal effort, the levels of educational achievement we set for all. Knowledge, abilities, attitudes are infinitely sharable, but honours and rewards by design are not. The hope is that by competing for the latter something of the former may also be gained. The justification would be that human nature rather than the nature of what is to be learned is what makes competition necessary here. Whereas children do not by nature seek to be educated, it will be said, fortunately they are naturally competitive.

Since I am at the moment concerned to explore what is possible rather than what is desirable, I shall leave the matter there and turn to a second main way in which competition can have a place in education. Children may want to be educated in some respect, but access to the necessary means may be restricted and have to be competed for. It is of course a familiar fact of social life that although knowledge is infinitely sharable, people may not be willing to share it. Teachers often jealously guard their ideas from the imitative intentions of colleagues. Researchers may set up a dummy scientific experiment to put others off the real scent. Trades and professions guard access to their special expertise and confer its benefits only at a price. Though knowledge is infinitely sharable, access to it can be restricted and artificially made an object of competition.

Now education is normally to be gained only by having access to certain institutions, where the attentions of teachers and the use of such equipment as books, laboratories and instruments is available. But these means represent very finitely sharable allocations of a community's resources. These allocations in turn reflect political decisions to train so many teachers and no more, to provide so many nursery, grammar school or university places and no more, and so on. With resources and access to them thus limited, competition for those resources and that access is certainly one way of distributing them.

When children leave their school and walk down the path or across the playground to the road outside, they take with them in varying degree that invisible but infinitely sharable achievement which we call being educated. But it is an achievement that has been made possible by having greater or less access to very finitely sharable resources, which can readily be made into objects of competition. In this way, as in motivating reluctant learners, competition can and often does have a place in education.

What things ought to be competed for?

In the previous section it was argued that competition can have an important place in education, both as a motivation for learning and as a means of determining access to educational resources. In turning finally to consider whether it ought to have either of these possible places, it is convenient to take first the simpler case of competition for access.

(a) Access

Concerning access, then, which is perhaps most obviously an issue at the ages of 11 and 18, there are two questions which need to be distinguished: (i) How much in the way of educational resources, e.g. university places, is it both possible and desirable to provide? (ii) If demand for access exceeds supply, how is entry to be determined? Now competition between pupils is relevant only to the second of these questions. Increase the educational provision and competition as a distributive device ceases to be necessary. The question of the merits and demerits of competition must therefore be separated from the prior and primarily political question of how much of our resources to allocate to some aspect of education.

Granted an excess of demand over supply, or a degree of scarcity of educational provision, competition is of course not the only way of determining access. The principle adopted could be that of first come first served, or random selection by lots, or teachers' recommendations, or being able to afford fees set so that only the required percentage can afford them. No doubt there are other possibilities too. But granted the institutional arrangements making selection necessary, then competition as a distributive device can be both the fairest and the most efficient. It can be fairest because it can most successfully restrict determination of the outcome to the candidate himself and his relevant abilities. And it can be most efficient because it can select those most able to profit from access to the resources provided. Furthermore, since the central point is to gain access, and only contingently to defeat rivals, then those aspects of triumphing over others and glorying in their defeat which may make competition objectionable for some are at least minimized if not wholly excluded.

It certainly seems to me that competition can be the most efficient way of allocating resources, but whether it is the fairest depends on one's conception of what it is necessary to be fair to. Competition is fair to the candidates as they now present themselves, but unfairness may lie behind how they now are, for instance in how they came to possess or be able to develop their present abilities. Tinkering with the system may partially satisfy an enlarged conception of fairness here, but serious doubts will almost certainly transfer the issue to the political question of how much educational provision to supply, i.e. it will by-pass the distributive device and bring into question the size or type of the institutions provided. And that is indeed another question.

(b) Motivation

The evaluation of competition as a motivation for learning is highly complex, and probably not in the end wholly rationally decidable. It is not just a question of accurately describing different sorts of competitive arrangements and then empirically discovering their different consequences. There is also the problem of knowing which consequences are to be relevant and what weights to attach to them. Whatever is officially approved, however, there will doubtless always be some unofficial competition between children: to be first on to Book Two, to have the biggest collection of fossils, to be most fashionable in hair or clothing, and so on. The question here is rather what a considered staff attitude should be. Competition is intrinsic to many games but it is not intrinsic to gaining possession of educational achievements, for these mental possessions are infinitely sharable. Should, therefore, a situation be artificially contrived in which children are moved to learn by the educationally extrinsic motivation of competitive success?

The use of competition in education is often defended by analogy with its approved place in games. A standard staffroom reply to the objector to competition is that he surely would not want it excluded from football, cricket, athletics or hockey. But how valid an analogy is this? Competitive games have two features which seem relevant here: (i) Competition is intrinsic to those games, and has indeed been deliberately introduced into them in order to make them more enjoyable. A game or sport can still be a good one through competing even if one loses. (To illustrate: I personally recall enjoying my first organized cross country race, in which I came 185th.) (ii) Playing games, in the spirit of a game, is voluntary, so that if one does not enjoy that sort of competition one can choose to stick to bird-watching, hiking or playing patience.

As an argument by analogy, however, this is unconvincing, for in both the respects mentioned educational learning frequently differs from games. First, as has already been argued, the intrinsic goals of education are non-competitive achievements with their own appropriate intrinsic motivations. Education is not a factitious goal set up just to provide an enjoyable field for the exercise and display of competitive skill and striving. Secondly, learners often do not have much choice as to whether or not to participate in the classroom arrangements which teachers institute. These, of course, are not by themselves objections to using competition in education, but to basing its use on an analogy with games and sports. Nevertheless, it must be admitted that there are some activities of learning in schools which may with great advantage be turned into games. If some tasteless pill of learning can be sugared by competition into being willingly taken, then why not? If some important spellings are thus learned, or some indispensable arithmetical facts are thus memorized, perhaps by minds which do not noticeably sparkle and flash with the intelligent perception of pattern or relation, then some good has been done which probably would not otherwise have been done. And if some children should occasionally choose to enter into a musical, painting or handwriting competition, then it would seem a doctrinaire restriction of liberty to stop them from doing so. But it is not these genuinely game-like activities which we have mainly to consider. What we have to consider, and what is not game-like, is the deliberate adoption of competitive arrangements in a school as a prime source of motivation for much educational learning.

And here, I think, at the heart of the matter lie different views of human nature. Where we find a classroom regime of competitive testing, class lists, comparative grading and ranking, prizes and other such rewards, then these will be upheld as a necessary spur to stimulate efficient learning and to 'keep up standards'. Without them, it will be said, children (and perhaps staff too) will flop back in to idleness and desultory learning. The argument can be developed by pointing out that competition has two great virtues which admirably suit it to this role of spurring on our slacking natures.

First, competitiveness is *natural*. The young display it without ever being taught, as we see in sibling rivalry. Such basic human endeavours as getting parental approval and attention and, later, getting sexual attention, automatically elicit a tendency to compete with any others who are seen as wanting the same attentions. Another aspect of this naturalness is that if it is suggested to children that they compete, then they very readily rise to the suggestion, competing the more vigorously the younger they are. No doubt cultures may have been heard of where non-competitiveness is regarded as a virtue, but again it could not be thought of as a *virtue* if competitiveness did not exist as a natural tendency to be curbed and controlled. Of course, simply being natural does not make anything desirable: selfish greed, jealousy, spite and envy are probably natural inclinations, but we do not approve of them on that or any other account. The argument is that because competitiveness is natural, it is available to serve as a means to learning, and it acquires value instrumentally from the value of what has to be learned.

Still further developing the argument, it may be said that a second admirable feature of competition is its wide applicability. It is like money. True, even with money you cannot buy a place in heaven, but you can buy a splendid funeral and the best plot in a cemetery, not to mention food, transport, entertainment, clothes, houses, works of art and promises. Rather similarly, such factitious goals of competitive success as getting prizes, coming top of the form, sitting in prestigeful seats and heading the star charts are attachable to the learning of anything that is learned alongside others, e.g. French, mathematics, history and even religious knowledge. And with such powerful arguments as these to make the case, one can then go on to point out certain additional bonuses. Through competition with others, it may be said, we come to know ourselves better and so form a truer self-concept, and we are prepared for what will later be a prevalent feature of much in adult life, especially in our work.

There are, I think, three possible moves open to anyone who wishes to oppose the general use of competition as a motivational device in education, and who therefore has to rebut the preceding arguments. The first and perhaps most obvious move would be to contest the facts relied upon in making the case for competition. It is not really necessary here to deny that competitiveness is natural. Suppose it could be shown that there are in fact *other* motivations available, perhaps just as natural. Then this would falsify the previous argument's implicit reliance on supposing competitiveness to be the only motivation available to accomplish the necessary learning. In the conveniently simplifying traditional or child-centred line-up of attitudes, competition is favoured by the traditionalist. But child-centred educationists would argue that children can be intrinsically motivated by educational learning and its standards as readily as they can be extrinsically motivated by competition. Furthermore, they can be motivated by less individualistic and more cooperative modes of learning, and by non-competitive personal goal-setting. More neutral in their partisan affiliations would be such further sources of motivation as perceived vocational utility, and the approval and encouragement of respected adults.

How could this seemingly factual dispute be settled? It might look as if a traditional teacher had only to try the alternative regime to determine its truth or falsity. But a common reaction to such a change is a confirmation of the traditionalist's fears. And a common further child-centred reaction to that apparent failure is that the children have for years had the old regime institutionally reinforced in them: they cannot change their nature overnight, and nor can the teacher change his. Now this dialogue really passes over into a distinct second move open to those who oppose competition. This move is to deny any significant fixity at all to 'human nature' in its relevant respects, and to assert instead that motivation follows upon rather than precedes the school's arrangements. Institutions make acting from some sorts of motive easy and acting from others difficult. They thus soon present a corresponding phenomenon of 'human nature' by a kind of Darwinian selection. Educationally formative institutions may therefore even be seen as subtly indoctrinatory in making it seem natural to suppose that people are inevitably of the nature that the institution itself engenders. Social psychological experiments into the different effects of different social climates show that there is at least some truth in the main propositions characteristic of this move. Yet these experiments never demonstrate the omnipotence of the experimenter. Limits and resistances to modifiability are found, though whether they are due to a core of genetic factors or to the effects of yet other institutions is unsettled.

There is yet a third possible move to make. This is broadly to accept the facts adduced by those who favour competition, but to argue that the consequences of adopting the practices based on those facts nevertheless do more harm than good. It may therefore overall be thought better to accept less efficient learning and some lowering of intellectual standards on account of the moral harm that is thus avoided. Whatever one thinks of this move, it does have the merit of explicitly drawing attention to what many people find objectionable in competition as a motivation. And the objection is not just that motivation is then extrinsic to the standards, skills and sensitivities of the educational goals that are set. After all, these may eventually become intrinsically motivating in the manner made familiar by Allport's principle of functional autonomy, e.g. we first go to sea for profit, but then come to love seafaring itself.

But there are strong moral objections, so far unheard, concerned with the effects of competition on interpersonal relationships. Roget's *Thesaurus* supplies the clue in classing competition under 'active antagonism', while Hobbes in the *Leviathan* placed it first amongst the three principal causes of quarrel among men.[3] Competition, it will be said, excludes many opportunities for cooperation. It stifles sympathies and erodes the sense of fraternity with our fellows. Seeing them as rivals, we see the price of their success as being our own self-esteem. Very naturally wishing to preserve that self-esteem, we are relieved by others' defeat, and even find ourselves glorying in others' failures. Emotions and attitudes towards others are engendered and released which are little, if at all, removed from malice, for others' loss may be our gain. And wanting to triumph over others can itself become functionally autonomous. In a predominantly competitive school regime, some must be unsuccessful and be consequently threatened by a general loss of self-esteem. To protect this, they will, if they do not despair, withdraw their concern from success in learning and locate it elsewhere. For competition will motivate learning only if there is some chance of relative success. One pointed way of putting this line of moral objection, then, is to ask where teachers can possibly get the right to organize the humiliation of some for the benefit of others, or to make it psychologically necessary for some to withdraw their concern from learning in order to preserve some self-esteem.

Not only are the issues involved in evaluating competition now seen to be complex beyond any hope of settling them in a single article, but also I think it must now be apparent that value-loadings and priorities may be differently distributed over this issue. It is doubtful whether the notion of 'the right answer' is applicable, though certainly many answers can be seen to be ill-considered, too narrow in what they take into account, based on false or dubious premises, or resting on doubtful presuppositions. Again, some of the bad effects of competition can in many ways be mitigated without abandoning competition altogether. For instance, if only the top five of thirty are identified, no one has the humiliation of being laughed at by classmates, or found a shameful disappointment by parents, for coming bottom of the class. These mitigating arrangements further prevent a final answer by blurring the issue.

The function of philosophy here, it seems to me, cannot therefore be to try to settle this question in just one way for everyone who will only attend to the arguments. Its function is rather the liberalizing one of drawing out presuppositions, clarifying concepts and examining validity. This can, I think, be liberalizing both in widening awareness of what is relevant to a personal decision, and in helping to create a larger field for reasoned discussion in place of what is often a rather bitter controversy. Small gains, it may be thought, if what we wanted was definitive solutions, but nevertheless gains for all that.

Notes and references

Chapter 1   Who should determine aims?

1 Central Advisory Council for Education (England), *Children and their Primary schools* (The Plowden Report), vol. 1, London: HMSO, 1967, chapter 15.
2 On this limitation of parental control, see my article 'How open can schools be?' in *Education 3–13*, vol. 2, no. 2, October 1974, pp. 88–93.
3 The case for a state-imposed curriculum is argued by J. P. White in his *Towards a Compulsory Curriculum*, London: Routledge & Kegan Paul, 1973.
4 See especially I. Illich, *De-schooling Society*, London: Calder & Boyars, 1971, and *After De-schooling, What?* London: Writers' and Readers' Publishing Cooperative, 1974.

Chapter 2   Aims and objectives

1 B. Bloom *et al.*, *Taxonomy of Educational Objectives*, Handbooks 1 and 2, London: Longmans, 1956.
2 L. Ennever *et al.*, *With Objectives in Mind*, London: Macdonald Educational, 1972.
3 See P. Ashton, 'What are primary teachers' aims?' in *Education 3–13*, vol. 1, no. 2, October 1973, pp. 91–7. A full account of the Aims of Primary Education Project later appeared in book form as P. Ashton, P. Keen, F. Davies and B. J. Holley, *The Aims of Primary Education: A Study of Teachers' Opinions*, London: Macmillan, 1975. But the much ampler statistics of the full report and the wider surveys which are also contained in it do nothing to answer the general criticisms of a survey approach made in this chapter. My concern with the project here, however, is less with its specific conclusions than it is with it as an illustration of one possible general approach to determining aims.
4 Sir Karl Popper, *The Poverty of Historicism*, London: Routledge & Kegan Paul, second edition 1960, preface.

Chapter 3 Curricular aims and curricular integration

1 Central Advisory Council for Education (Wales), *Primary Education in Wales* (The Gittins Report), London: HMSO, 1967, p. 191.
2 See P. H. Hirst, *Knowledge and the Curriculum,* London: Routledge & Kegan Paul, 1974.

Chapter 4 Child-centred education

1 A. S. Neill, 'Freedom Works' in P. Adams *et al., Children's Rights,* London: Elek Books, 1971, p. 129.

Chapter 5 The concept of teaching

1 B. F. Skinner, *The Technology of Teaching,* New York: Appleton-Century-Crofts, 1968, p. 5.
2 I. Scheffler, *Reason and Teaching,* London: Routledge & Kegan Paul, 1973, p. 67.
3 P. H. Hirst and R. S. Peters, *The Logic of Education,* London: Routledge & Kegan Paul, 1970, chapter 5.

Chapter 6 Learning how to learn and learning by discovery

1 H. F. Harlow, 'The Formation of Learning Sets', in *Psychological Review,* vol. 56, 1948, pp. 51–65.
2 H. F. Harlow, 'Learning to Think' in E. Stones (ed.), *Readings in Educational Psychology,* London: Methuen, 1970, p. 7
3 *Ibid.,* p. 8.
4 F. Musgrove, 'The Contribution of Sociology to the Study of the Curriculum', in J. Kerr (ed.), *Changing the Curriculum,* London: University of London Press, 1963, p. 105.
5 L. Sealey and V. Gibbon, *Communication and Learning in the Primary School,* Oxford: Blackwell, 1962, p. 17.
6 N. Postman and C. Weingartner, *Teaching as a Subversive Activity,* Harmondsworth: Penguin, 1971, p. 99.
7 Central Advisory Council for Education (England), *Children and their Primary Schools* (The Plowden Report), vol. 1, London: HMSO, 1967, para. 529.
8 Central Advisory Council for Education (Wales), *Primary Education in Wales* (The Gittins Report), London: HMSO, 1967, sect. 10.3.
9 I am indebted for this distinction to H. T. Sockett, 'Curriculum Aims and Objectives: Taking a Means to an End' in *Proceedings of the Philosophy of Education Society,* vol. 6, no. 1, 1972, pp. 30–61.
10 B. Bloom *et al., Taxonomy of Educational Objectives,* Handbook 1, London: Longmans, 1956, p. 32.

Chapter 7   What is the integrated day?

1 L. Marsh, *Alongside the Child,* London: Black, 1970.
2 M. Brown and N. Precious, *The Integrated Day in the Primary School,* London: Ward Lock Educational, 1968.
3 D. Hawkins, 'Square Two, Square Three', in *Forum,* vol. 12, no. 1, autumn 1969, pp. 4–9.
4 R. F. Dearden, *The Philosophy of Primary Education,* London: Routledge & Kegan Paul, 1968, chapter 4.

Chapter 8   Reading and research

1 H. P. Smith and E. V. Dechant, *Psychology in Teaching Reading,* Englewood Cliffs, N. J.: Prentice-Hall, 1961, p. 213.
2 P. H. Hirst, 'Liberal Education and the Nature of Knowledge', in R. D. Archambault (ed.), *Philosophical Analysis and Education,* London: Routledge & Kegan Paul, 1965.
3 R. S. Peters, *Ethics and Education,* London: Allen & Unwin, 1966, part 1.
4 J.-J. Rousseau, *Emile,* 1972 (Everyman Edition), p. 123.
5 S. Hampshire, *Thought and Action,* London: Chatto & Windus, 1959, p. 40.

Chapter 9   Competition in education

1 I stress that this third condition is necessary only if A and B are consciously to compete. But it might be said that conditions one and two are together sufficient, without condition three, in cases of unconscious competition, as in applying for a job in ignorance of the fact that there are other applicants. This distinction might be called that between 'objective' and 'subjective' competition. But condition two, concerning exclusiveness, is the most interesting of the three, I think, and is common to both objective and subjective competition.
2 Spinoza, *Ethics,* 1677, part 4, proposition 36.
3 Hobbes, *Leviathan,* 1651, part 1, chapter 13.

Index

Index